THE
Art of
HURLING

DAIRE WHELAN

THE
Art of
HURLING

INSIGHTS INTO SUCCESS FROM THE MANAGERS

MERCIER PRESS
IRISH PUBLISHER – IRISH STORY

For Charlie, who has taught me so much already about never giving up and never giving in.

Nearly all men can stand adversity, but if you want to test a man's character, give him power.

Abraham Lincoln

MERCIER PRESS

Cork

www.mercierpress.ie

ISBN: 978 1 78117 481 4

10 9 8 7 6 5 4 3 2 1

A CIP record for this title is available from the British Library

Printed and bound in the EU.

CONTENTS

INTRODUCTION

'A simple game made complicated by the coaches' was how some former managers put it. Learn to lift, strike, block, catch, throw in a bit of instinct and character and there you have it, your secret sauce to the 'art of hurling'. Sure, if you simply stick to your position, are first to the ball and have enough determination about you, you'll win the game.

But is it really as simple as that? Are modern-day coaches complicating things for the sake of it, throwing in drills, science, stats and game plans where they're not needed?

The game is neither as simple as sepia-tinted memories would have it, nor as complicated as PhD statistics graduates want to make it. Instead, the reality is somewhere in between the two ends of this spectrum.

But we also have to accept that the 'modern' techniques being decried, such as statistics, possession and changing formations, have all been used in one form or another down through the decades. It's just that they have become more developed, increasingly codified and, with more information and knowledge around them, they've become studies in themselves. Such developments don't make these techniques wrong, just more advanced.

You don't throw the baby out with the bath water because

something is more 'advanced', and the new solutions being offered are not the be all and end all. They are not, in and of themselves, the answer or the key to winning matches.

Having worked in the media in all its forms in the last fifteen years, I think of the times when new types of media were developed and introduced and how people were quick to declare each one of them the new and only way media would be consumed, pronouncing the death of whatever had come before it. Radio would spell the end of newspapers; TV would be the end of radio; the Internet would be the end of everything.

Likewise, when increased fitness and science were being introduced to the championship in hurling and football in the late 1980s/early 1990s, we were told that this would finally level the playing field. Indeed, the breakthrough of Ulster teams in Gaelic football and the 'revolution years' in hurling in the 1990s did offer a glimpse of a possible new order being established in both codes. But in truth it was only a brief hiatus before the traditionally dominant counties reasserted themselves, as they caught up with whatever new coaching/science/system was in vogue, applied it to their own supremely talented numbers and watched the positive results follow.

It wasn't as simple as that, of course, but evolutions in both codes occur in cycles as new thinking, new influences and new information come on stream. Kilkenny legend Fr Tommy Maher, 'the godfather of modern hurling', learned about training techniques from English soccer; Down's Joe

Lennon and Dublin's Kevin Heffernan in Gaelic football were likewise bringing in lessons learned from 'foreign games'.

The 1960s were the tipping point in the GAA's coaching evolution. Previously it was sporadic and haphazard, based on individuals and what they brought to a team at any given time. Now, for the first time, figures such as Maher, Donie Nealon of Tipperary and others were codifying and instructing how Gaelic games should be coached. They were also organising residential, week-long 'instructional' courses in Gormanston, Co. Meath during the 1960s, where the next generation of hurling and football coaches would be created.

My first interviewee, Diarmuid Healy, learned at Gormanston and was also taught directly by Tommy Maher at St Kieran's College in Kilkenny, that famous nursery of hurling for secondary-school students. He was one of the first pupils to come out of the modern school of hurling coaching in Gormanston. He emphasised skills over physique, finesse over brute force, and his results with St Kieran's, the Kilkenny minors and then Offaly showed that this approach worked. Offaly, a county with no Leinster or All-Ireland titles to its name, was to win provincial and national titles for the first time in its history under Healy's influence.

Cyril Farrell was another thirty-something-year-old who learned about the art of management from outside sources. In his case, he absorbed information from the New Zealand rugby team and Shamrock Rovers soccer team on his way to ending Galway's fifty-seven-year hurling famine.

Although neither Farrell nor Healy ever reached inter-county standard themselves as players, both men were avid students of sport. They were sponges, soaking up any new information from all sporting codes and then applying it to hurling.

But former inter-county stars were also just as likely to make it as All-Ireland-winning managers – Justin McCarthy, Ger Loughnane, Anthony Daly and Brian Cody to name but a few. They were as hungry for sports management tips and techniques as the others, except they probably had it a little easier. They could walk into a dressing room and command respect from players who knew who they were and what they had achieved.

As I sought out some of hurling's most successful managers for this book, what I wanted were their insights into and philosophies about how they achieved what they achieved. In most instances the effect they had on a team was immediate, or it became apparent within a season or two.

Longevity is not a common trait amongst the majority of successful managers. After shining so brightly so quickly, they were almost certainly gone within a few years. And for those who go back a second time after an absence of ten or more years, the advice is clear: don't do it. Rarely does it work out. Time passes, generations and society move on, and what worked twenty years ago now needs updating with new methods and new techniques and a new voice to make it relevant and have an impact.

It's no coincidence that many of the managers who made the most impact were in their thirties, just old enough to be the senior of most players, but still close enough to be able to relate to whatever was preoccupying their lives and hurling styles.

New methods have been brought to bear by the newer generation of coaches interviewed for this book. New ways of training, new playing styles and new coaching techniques introduced to the hurling field can be either accepted or ridiculed. One sure-fire way of these methods gaining acceptance in any group, however, is by winning. Success breeds confidence and surety, and, all of a sudden, sceptical voices in a dressing room become the methods' biggest evangelists.

Just as Mike Brearley, in his book *The Art of Captaincy*, brings us insights into being a captain in cricket and signals the importance of a captain's decision-making, these hurling managers reveal what it was like to hold the flame for a few seasons in their beloved sport.

If you were to pick one singular trait that stands out throughout each of the interviews in this book, it is that of a strong mentality and mindset. An increasingly popular refrain in the modern workplace is that you hire on attitude because skills can be learned afterwards. So too in the dressing room. It's a trait that managers have long known about and looked for. When counties make the breakthrough after losing for so many years, they point to mindset and belief as being the determining factor.

Skill sets at third level, we're told throughout the book, are on a par between players from top-tier and weaker counties. They're playing against each other on a regular basis in colleges, with little discernible difference. But when they go to play for their counties, where tradition, history and the jersey itself count for so much, something in the mentality can change. Circumstances, players and the pitch can all be the same, but the belief within the players from the weaker counties just dissipates when they're on the county scene.

Since belief can be such a fickle thing, the importance of the managers' role as psychologists and leaders is clear. They have to be able to connect with the players they have chosen to bring success to the team; they have to know what makes them tick, what's going on in their lives, what will inspire them to get out of the trenches and push themselves to the limit.

But it also has to come from within – which is why the choice of players is so important. It's something that Terence 'Sambo' McNaughton alludes to when discussing his latest stint as Antrim manager. The county doesn't have the resources or playing numbers to compete as they once used to. Instead, he has to find players who want it that much more, players who desperately want to avoid the bitter taste of defeat, because, as Cyril Farrell said after Galway's 1979 All-Ireland final defeat, 'it hurts so bad they don't want to go through that feeling ever again'.

Character looms large for former Clare and Galway

manager Ger Loughnane. 'Men needed now' should be on his calling card. He didn't want the most skilful or silkiest hurlers. He wanted the ones who would do what it took, no matter what. Loughnane's method for choosing his inter-county players was akin in many ways to the likes of the induction courses for the elite Navy Seals special ops groups. The gruelling, punishing ordeal he put recruits through was not about the physical torture; instead the mental strength of every individual was being tested. Could they put themselves through this much hurt and still not give up, no matter what?

Not many can at that level. Though, of course, you can get through numerous boot camps and still not be good enough. Just because you can climb Carrantuohill in your bare feet in the middle of winter with a 40lb pack on your back and nothing but rain and cold for company for twenty-four hours, doesn't mean you will win an All-Ireland.

People are increasingly asking, however, is this not push-ing it too far? Is this what we're saying is needed now to win in an amateur sport? Ice baths are no longer seen as cutting edge or advanced. If you're not doing them there are questions asked. They're now as normal as stretching your hamstrings in the warm-up.

Then, just when you think the body can't be pushed any more, new ways and methods are found and implemented, and if a county wins an All-Ireland using them, well then you can be sure the other counties will be doing something similar for the following season.

The Internet has brought increased access to information from all sports, which is shared amongst coaches and clubs across the sporting landscape. Rather than going to Ajax to study their Total Football system, they can instead download it in seconds from the web, and the same information is available to every other coach out there looking for it.

For how much longer can a one per cent edge be found? The days of other sporting influences bringing something different are no more, and the limits of physical endurance have been pushed to the extreme, which leaves the mind as the last frontier left to develop. That's why you hear coaches around the world in different sports from New Zealand to America to Ireland talking about character. It's that X factor, that unquantifiable element that makes a person push and drive themselves on. It comes from within, it comes from having lived, fallen down and gotten up again. It comes from learning about life and wanting to succeed when everyone else gives up.

To paraphrase the self-help gurus' mantra: when you discover the 'why' of life (or sport), then the 'how' doesn't even matter. But in an amateur sport such as hurling, accepting why you persevere in the sport, especially later in life, can become more difficult as it begins to interfere with family, career and kids. After all, you win a few All-Irelands and then what? In ten years' time will anyone really care if you've given up your future prospects to focus on hurling?

The counter to that, as many of the managers in this book

note, is that the same attitude, purpose and drive you bring to your hurling career should also be reflected in your life outside of that. And if you bring the same drive to your job or business or family, then life will fall into place.

But what if the huge dedication and time commitments required for training, strength and conditioning, diet and playing are causing inter-county players to miss out on what life can actually teach them? Is modern sport creating automatons on the field, only able to carry out instructions but little else besides? What can they bring to life, career and family in such circumstances?

All of the managers featured in this book come from generations where they switched on for hurling but also knew when to switch off. Pints could be had, days afterwards lost in a fog. The craic, mistakes, highs and lows were all part of it. Team life ebbed and flowed, up and down, up and down. Now it's all tightly controlled, driven by the minute, the schedule and the goals. It's militaristic. To succeed, the mindset of an army cadet is a better fit than ever before.

Is it any wonder that perhaps the most successful Gaelic football side of all time, the current Dublin side, is managed by Jim Gavin, a former Air Corps pilot? He has said his military background has been instrumental to his leadership in the dressing room. 'Service not self. In the military there's people above you and below but you're there to serve.' Tellingly, however, Gavin also said they don't want players as robots on the field. 'We give them a framework in a tactical sense, we don't want fifteen robots playing for Dublin. We have a structure, sometimes we get it wrong but once they express themselves that's the key.' Maybe that piece of understanding is the one per cent difference for the Dubs at the moment.

It comes back to the balance. Not being too systems-driven, but on the other hand, not being too much of a keep-it-simple merchant either. If Gavin has got it right for Dublin in Gaelic football, then Brian Cody has been the undoubted master in hurling terms. With his longevity and success, he is the Alex Ferguson of the GAA, and the worry for Kilkenny, with the rising dominance of other sides, is: what happens when Cody is gone?

Time and again, the managers in this book cited Kilkenny and Cody as the exemplars which every other county has to follow. If Fr Tommy Maher was the original godfather of hurling, then Cody has been his successor for the twenty-first century. His influence, his success, his ability to mould and shape not only the players but a culture of success breeding success is what stands out for every hurling manager past, present and future.

Tellingly, Cody wouldn't be interviewed for this book. While he's still managing, a former manager told me, he won't talk. 'He's not going to want to talk to you about his methods and how he made Kilkenny so successful, certainly not while he's still in the game.'

I had to accept this and I'm sure when Cody does step down he'll have another book ready for the shelves. As with

Ferguson in retirement, it is likely that most people will be most interested in his nuggets of advice about management and leadership. Who knows, maybe the *Cody Book of Leadership* will be the next book to come?

In the meantime, all everyone else can do is sit back and respect what has been achieved in his nearly twenty years with Kilkenny. As it was with Ferguson, so too will it be with Cody. We will likely never see a managerial career like that in Gaelic games again. The intensity, the pressure, the commitments are all too much and by the end of the third season most, if not all, managers are ready to jump ship.

This book is not trying to be an all-encompassing or definitive work on hurling managers. Such a book would need to run to numerous volumes to include the many, many managers not interviewed here, from counties to clubs, and it would, of course, need to include Cody himself.

Besides, there are plenty of other books already published that profile the game's top managers. What *The Art of Hurling* tries to do is offer insights into the philosophies and methodologies of some of the game's most successful managers. They are the ones who not only won All-Irelands or provincial titles, but did so in unique circumstances, often ending decades-long losing streaks and most times bringing success within a season or two of taking over.

How were they able to take losing teams and turn them into champions in such a short space of time? What was it about their philosophies and beliefs on the game and the dressing room that made them unique and successful? And finally, in the midst of such a period of reflection about the game and its development, what are their thoughts on the future of hurling?

It was with these themes in mind that the managers were approached for interview, although a geographical spread was also a factor, as was inter-county success. There's another volume in club managers alone, and another for those whose lights shone brightly with smaller counties.

Each chapter then is a study about the manager, their philosophy and the implementation of that philosophy during their managerial career. Their successes (or otherwise) are the anchor points along their journey (and the teams'). Can one word sum up their lifetime commitment to the sport? Perhaps not, but each chapter is meant as a stand-alone essay reflecting an overall belief or theme, so that readers can pick up and dip into it as they so desire.

There is also a roughly chronological path, from Diarmuid Healy, who began his inter-county managerial career in 1979, to Eamon O'Shea, who ended his tenure as Tipperary manager in 2015. One can trace the changing landscape in hurling coaching in general as one reads about the successes of the 1980s into the 1990s and the twenty-first century.

Looking to the future, there are some who are fearful for the game, while others see only improved facilities, fitness and skills.

It is fascinating, however, to trace the increased influence of player power in later years, and the expectancy that managers should treat players, if not quite as equals, then certainly as important voices in the make-up of a team's approach.

One also sees managers trying to bring a sense of balance and expression to players' sporting lives. There is an awareness that, with demands on players at an all-time high, they need to be introduced positively to other outlets, to other areas beyond the pitch. However, it still ultimately comes down to a love of the game, pride of community, club and county for the players, and for the managers, it is clear that their love of hurling remains undiminished.

They are more than just managers, they are also the guardians of how the game should be played, shining examples of how success and All-Irelands can be brought to a county, so their philosophies and approach should be seen in that context. If they're lucky, their legacy in these counties will live on and count for the generations to come. And that is the true art of hurling.

1

Technique:
DIARMUID HEALY

If you miss a ball, it's just another opportunity for why you should win the next one.

A common refrain heard these days is that it's harder than it used to be to manage a team to an All-Ireland, particularly outside of the traditional 'superpowers'. Look back on the history books and records of most sports, however, and it is clear that just a handful of teams have always dominated – the Dublins, Kerrys, Man Utds, Barcelonas, Kilkennys, Corks and Tipperarys.

But we've had – and do still have – occasional breaks in teams' hegemonies. It might only be brief before sporting empires reassert themselves, but it can still happen. There was the Leicester Premier League fairytale and Connacht's Pro12 rugby success in 2016; there were the Ulster Gaelic football breakthroughs in the 1990s, followed by the hurling 'revolution years' in the same decade with the All-Ireland wins for traditional hurling minnows Offaly, Clare and Wexford from 1994–98. It was a breakthrough decade and brought so much colour, joy and surprise to the sport that the game of hurling was rejuvenated and reawakened. At the time, people wondered was this to be the future of the sport, whereby the 'smaller' counties had now caught up with the big guns. While the Clares, Wexfords and Offalys were dominating, there was a brief glimpse of what hurling's new order might look like.

But in order to succeed, revolutions have to bring about long-lasting change that establishes the new order. For these counties, their stars shone brightly for a moment and then faded away just as quickly. After Offaly's win over Kilkenny in the 1998 All-Ireland, it was to be another fifteen years before someone other than Cork, Tipperary or Kilkenny would win an All-Ireland. That was Clare's surprise 2013 win, but in the years since it has once again been primarily Kilkenny and Tipp slugging it out.

Kilkenny's dominance under Brian Cody has been un-precedented, both for the duration of their dominance and for how far they pulled away from the rest of the country. Of their eight All-Ireland final victories from 2006–15, only Cork in 2006 and Tipp in 2015 were within three points of them at the final whistle.

'You'll never see years like the 1990s again' is another common refrain heard in hurling circles. There is a general feeling that the top counties have pulled so far ahead that the gap to the smaller counties is too far, too insurmountable, for breakthrough surprises to occur any more.

Are the days of the minnows sometimes toppling the kingpins gone in hurling, or at least becoming even rarer? In the face of money, sponsorship, commercial nous, stats and science, will upsets eventually become a thing of the past?

It is worth then, in the midst of the modern game where Kilkenny's incredible dominance has forced many counties to look at themselves again, considering a time when a county without a history of provincial hurling titles – never mind All-Irelands – was able to pierce the Kilkenny hegemony. Although this was in the days before the introduction of the backdoor system in 1997, which meant once you were out, you were out, this was a county that still succeeded without the resources and knowledge of traditionally dominant county set-ups. The fact that it was a Kilkenny man who made it happen is probably no coincidence.

Diarmuid Healy's years as manager of Offaly saw them reach three All-Irelands in the five years from 1981 to 1985 (winning in 1981 and 1985) and compete in every Leinster final in the 1980s (winning six). It was a remarkable achievement for a county that had never reached an All-Ireland final in their history before this period and, in provincial terms, had never won a Leinster title and had only been in five finals.

This wasn't a reawakening by a Clare or a Wexford, a Waterford or a Galway, teams with previous experience of winning All-Irelands. This was Offaly coming out of nowhere to shake up the established order and you could argue that, in doing so, they enabled the breakthrough years for the rest of the 'little' counties in the 1990s. Offaly set the benchmark and proved it could be done, giving a glimmer of hope to others who felt they could follow in their footsteps.

If Offaly's success came as a total surprise, the phone call in 1979 to appoint the manager who was to lead them was also a surprise to the man himself.

'I thought it was someone having me on. I never had any great ambitions,' Diarmuid Healy explains. 'I had been involved with St Kieran's College and the Kilkenny minors during the '70s when we won several All-Ireland titles. Each year we came back after winning, people would be saying, "Something must be done about hurling in the weaker counties." But none of us were doing anything about it and then when I got this phone call from the Offaly County Board, I said, "Yeah, this is a challenge."'

While Kilkenny and Cork shared out All-Irelands between them in the 1970s, the question was could it be done outside of the big counties?

Healy was only thirty-one when he got the phone call, but he had been managing teams since he was nineteen. He was in the seminary, training to be a priest at the time, when Kilkenny's hurling guru, Fr Tommy Maher, asked him to help coach the teams in St Kieran's College. Over the years Maher would come down and watch him coaching, giving a few pieces of advice.

TECHNIQUE: DIARMUID HEALY

Tommy Maher obviously saw something in Healy, even at that young age, because two years later, at just twenty-one, he was managing St Kieran's to an All-Ireland before looking after the Kilkenny minors all through his twenties.

For a student of the game, to have Maher teaching you the rudiments of coaching was perhaps the best foundation of all. Maher was regarded as one of the most influential hurling coaches of all time, taking Kilkenny to twelve All-Ireland finals in eighteen seasons (winning seven) from 1957 to 1975. Maher's influence was far-reaching, with Brian Cody also playing for and learning from him.

The coaching of Gaelic games was being taken more seriously from the 1960s on, when the likes of Joe Lennon in Gaelic football and Tommy Maher, Donie Nealon, John Hanley and Ned Power in hurling began to organise the famous Gormanston coaching courses. These courses were the precursor to the current coaching system in the GAA, with their focus on developing a more scientific approach to the game, as well as proper teaching and understanding of the skills of the game. It was revolutionary at the time and Healy attended the courses, soaking up all this new information.

'Fr Tommy Maher was very progressive and he saw the need for coaching,' says Healy. 'Coaching in the GAA at that time was heresy. When they drew up a syllabus for the course in Gormanston, they submitted it to the GAA Central Council, who agreed to the course going ahead, but with one proviso – that it couldn't be called a coaching course. It was to be a "hurling instructional course" instead.

'The course was residential and it was absolutely fantastic. You went into a classroom and the four boys broke down the game into the skills. They talked about how to catch the ball, lifting the ball, striking the ball. They discussed that in the classroom for three-quarters of an hour, and then you went out onto the field for another three-quarters of an hour and implemented it. They went through all the skills like that for the week. It was just fantastic and that was my introduction and background in it.'

With Maher overseeing his coaching and then being able to put it into practice with St Kieran's, Healy's apprenticeship was developed in ideal circumstances. As he had only played intermediate hurling in Kilkenny, Healy was able to concentrate on his coaching career and was soon proving himself under Maher's watchful eye.

His youth wasn't an impediment either, although it's always easier to get buy-in from the players when your methods prove successful.

'When I started changing things, luckily the changes worked,' he says. 'The emphasis was on game skills, emphasising the skill rather than the physical game and suddenly players saw themselves improving. They said to themselves, "This lad must know something", so they began to listen more and improve.'

It sounds simple but, for Healy, it was about taking the

game back to basics and improving players in each of its constituent parts. Even at county level, when he joined Offaly, he would be showing them how to lift and strike the ball properly. And even though players are being coached from such a young age nowadays, he still believes there's a need for the coaching of skills to be continuous and ongoing.

'People go to coaching courses and they're given drills, to do this, to do that, but they don't know how to apply them when they go back with the team. Now I see some clubs telling me that a training session is a series of drills and nothing else. The most I would do any night in a training session with drills would be to implement something, such as a specific skill like the block. Knowing when to apply it and implement it in a training session is a huge problem that I see.

'I see it in Kilkenny here as well. Players are getting the ball and there could be a loose man up in the forwards from 50 yards away, but no, they hit the ball to the nearest player because that's all they're doing in drill situations. You get the ball, hit it to the nearest lad and then he hits it back to you. They're conditioned in training, they could be spending an hour doing these drills. They're not thinking, "Oh, there's a lad up in corner-forward on his own."'

While at the elite county level skills have improved on previous generations, he says at club level it's going down and that what you sometimes see in club matches can be terrible.

'Give them the basics. My attitude always was to make sure each player perfects all the skills that can be done. People say, "That guy can't do this or can't do that", but every player can perform all the skills and can perfect them. If you've all your players with the skills perfected, then you'll be able to belt that ball up to the corner-forward. But the flair has gone out of the game and we're losing something with that.'

When the call from Offaly came out of the blue in 1979, Healy was intrigued enough to sit down and meet with the county board. He wanted to see what they'd think of his ideas. Would they be open to how he wanted to coach? He also wanted to see what they were expecting from him. The meeting went well and Offaly officials wanted what he could bring. But only just. Offaly had never gone for an outside coach before, but at the end of 1979 the county board narrowly voted for change and Healy was duly appointed. The county had just won the Leinster U-21 hurling title the previous year – it was Offaly's first ever Leinster hurling title at any level – and they knew they had promising young players coming through. They needed someone who had a track record of coaching successful youth sides and Healy was the perfect fit.

After all the years coaching colleges and minors, it was going to be quite the step up to senior level, especially with a county that had no track record in hurling. He was going to be given a chance to prove himself and his years of learning would be put to the test.

The Offaly set-up back then wasn't quite like the autonomous set-up experienced by modern managers. Healy had five selectors alongside him, although for the eight years he was there it was the same set-up and disagreements over team selection never reached a stage where a vote had to be taken amongst them. The coaching dynamic was driven by consensus, discussion and persuasion.

It was unique, though, to have this thirty-one-year-old from Kilkenny in charge, but he was determined to have things done his way, whether or not it was the done thing. There was none of this choosing the team the night before a match to keep the players on their toes; instead Healy and his selectors would agree on the starting fifteen amongst themselves a full three weeks before the big games.

Each night following the selection would be a constant review between Healy and the selectors, changing and adjusting things if required. It was pointless, Healy believed, announcing the team at the last minute. Players had to be coached as to the requirements in their positions for game time and the weeks leading up to the game was the time for the starting line-up to work on and perfect their play.

However, the team wasn't so settled that players could rest on their laurels for the three weeks leading up to a match. 'If you weren't going well in training then you might not be in the same position the next night and suddenly you're thinking and wondering, "Am I not going to make it now?"' Though Healy is quick to add that they barely had the numbers to get fifteen on the pitch in the first place, so they didn't have the luxury of two to three players fighting for every position.

He knew the challenge he was facing all right. But at least

his home-county people had given their blessing when he went to Offaly. Offaly were never going to be rivals, Kilkenny figured, so Healy's move couldn't hurt them.

For Healy, he was going to Offaly to promote the game, to see if he could improve the lot of hurling in a smaller county and help bring future generations into the sport. The team had been doing well in the league off the back of the successful U-21s, but no one was expecting miracles in the short term. When Healy arrived, he wanted to know what type of training they were doing and wasn't unduly surprised when he saw the emphasis was mainly placed on the physical side of the game. It was like a throwback to the time before Tommy Maher and his cohorts introduced the new way of thinking into the game via the Gormanston courses. Their message, it seemed, hadn't reached Offaly.

This was Healy's opportunity to implement the lessons learned in Gormanston in the real world, away from the manuals and the classroom.

Offaly's past teams were known for hard play, giving away frees and bottling it when it got tight at the end. Healy quickly looked to work on these issues. He immediately changed how the players trained, focusing on the skills and not the physical. It might have seemed simplistic and back to basics, but that was what was required and it was Healy's philosophy. One of his first moves was to introduce lighter hurleys, thus allowing the players greater flexibility and freedom.

'We stopped fouling,' Offaly's centre back, Pat Delaney,

told *The Sunday Times'* Denis Walsh. 'It was hook, hassle, twist them, turn them, block them.'

'He brought a different thinking,' Offaly defender Pat Fleury also told Walsh. 'You didn't need a King Cobra driver to clear the ball, a nine-iron would get it away just as good. The lighter hurleys helped to make you more wristy. All these things hadn't been brought to our attention before.'

Healy says, 'I always tell people you can't have a hurley either too light or too short. With the long, heavy hurley, the swing just sickens. I brought up a few of the lighter ones and gradually a couple of them began to use them. But what really convinced them was when we played Laois in a match and we had to get a point from about eighty yards to draw the game. Paddy Kirwan was one of the people who had the light hurleys and he took the free and it sailed over the bar. After that, they all tried to get a hurl from me. That was it. With the light hurleys you get the quick flick and I always said, the quick flick gets you out into open spaces with the ball.'

Get them to perfect the skills and everything would fall into place; this was Healy's thinking. Afterwards, Offaly started moving the ball fast, 'shocking fast' according to Healy, and were, if anything, taking on Kilkenny at their own game. The players were learning new skills and they learned quickly. With the likes of Delaney and Fleury leading the players in the dressing room, they embraced the change.

'They were an intelligent group,' says Healy. 'And if you've an intelligent group, it solves half of your problems. I didn't have to be telling them the same things every night. They were all leaders on their own. We often had brainstorming sessions and the notes would come out at those and the criticism could be hot and heavy.

'We had great sessions where they weren't afraid to criticise each other and then afterwards it was no problem. I often said if an outsider listened in, they'd say those lads would never talk to one another. But you have to get them thinking for themselves. You have to be asking them, "What would you do in this situation, and why didn't that happen there?" Now, there's times when you just have to walk through a lad, literally, but generally you lead them along and bring them with you.'

So much of it is reminiscent of Kevin Heffernan's approach with the Dubs, of whom Healy was a great admirer. He'd call upon Heffernan for coaching and training advice from time to time. Heffernan had been the saviour of Dublin football in the 1970s, taking over a team that couldn't win in Leinster and leading them to become one of the most exciting and successful sides in the history of Gaelic football.

Once, after Offaly drew a game and had a week to the replay, Healy rang Heffernan to get his thoughts on the training he wanted the players to do.

'If a team goes out and does heavy physical training in between, you often see replays that can be totally one-sided; that's because that team has done the wrong thing,' says Healy. 'I rang Heffernan that night and he'd been at the match, and he said it was a tough match and to take it easy. I told him we're going to do a half an hour puck around on Tuesday night, and half an hour on Thursday night. Heffernan's response was, "I'd make it twenty-five minutes." That convinced me I was doing the right thing.'

Healy points out that, with the players, a lot of it was mental. Where before they would have been losing by a point, suddenly, with this newfound confidence in their skill set and training, they were now winning games by a point.

'Ninety per cent of it was psychological,' he believes. 'The first year I was there, it was coming up to Christmas and there had been a big article in the Sunday papers about who's going to win next year's All-Ireland. I thought I'd see how the players would react to this, so as we were talking one night after training, I said to them, "Did you see the paper today, lads? Who do you think is going to do it?" They named out every team except Offaly. "Lads, when you're finished changing," I told them, "we're going to have a meeting." And then for about half an hour I beat the balls off them. "What am I doing here? What are you doing here?" I asked, fuming at them. "Not one of you mentioned the possibility that you could win an All-Ireland!"

'The truth was, I saw the possibility. They were winning league matches, they beat Kilkenny and they were doing well. I saw what they could achieve. It was based on reality, but if they weren't setting their sights then it was pointless. But it just got them thinking on a different level. And from then on they began to discuss it and think about an All-Ireland as a possibility and I kept reinforcing that all the time with them.'

What really set it in motion for them was when, in Healy's first season in 1980, they reached their first Leinster final since 1969. They faced his own county, Kilkenny, who were not only going for three-in-a-row in Leinster, but were also the reigning All-Ireland champions.

'I went out during the minor match and the late Mick Dunne [RTÉ's first GAA correspondent] came over to me. "Well, how are you going to do?" he asked. He was probably expecting me to say that we'll be in trouble or something like that, but I turned to him and said, "We're going to win today, Mick" and within a minute he was gone from me. It was only afterwards that John Dowling told me that Dunne went over to him and said, "Is Healy mad?" That was the perception of Offaly hurling at the time.'

A crowd of only 9,613 were in Croke Park that day. Nobody expected anything but a Kilkenny win. Kilkenny were going for their forty-ninth provincial title; Offaly had never beaten Kilkenny in the championship in their history. How would it be any different this time?

Despite coming out of the blocks and building up a lead over the reigning champions, by half-time Offaly were trailing. The next thirty-five minutes looked like it would be the same old story.

Except this time, Healy wasn't letting his team out of that dressing room until he was sure that the players were certain they would win. They had to believe. It was the only thing holding them back. GAA officials were banging on the door, Kilkenny were back out on the pitch waiting for them, but Healy still wouldn't let up.

The next thirty-five minutes were to change Offaly hurling history and create one of the sport's great rivalries for the next twenty years, as Offaly shook off the shackles of their own history and stood up to Kilkenny, seeing it through to the end and winning by just a single point. That second-half performance was everything they had never been, it was everything that Healy had seen in them.

This performance came from a culture and mindset that Healy created from the day he arrived, one where everyone was only thinking of winning. Early on in his reign as they walked off the pitch after losing a challenge match, one of his selectors said, 'Oh, typical Offaly, back in the arse of the garden.'

Healy turned on him. 'We're not back in the feckin' arse of the garden. We have to think positive all the time, this is just a hiccup, we'll win the next day.' Anyone that talked negatively would be cut down immediately.

Now Offaly had beaten Kilkenny for the first time in the championship and were the Leinster hurling champions for the first time in their county's history. Could it get any better?

Some might say an All-Ireland would have done nicely, but Galway beat them in the semi-final before going on to win the Liam MacCarthy Cup. Healy believes that it would have been too much too soon.

'It didn't all come suddenly, it was just a stepping stone, which was a good thing. I was afraid even when we got into the league final the following year because we didn't train hard for that league and Cork beat us well in the end. We could say then, "Lads, at least we got to a league final and it's a stepping stone."'

Wintertime was just about ticking over. There was no hard discipline on the players and the league wasn't much on their minds. Once March came around, however, it was back to the serious stuff.

'They knew it was serious and they got down to it then. With a limited pool of players, if you're constantly on their backs all the time you'll wear them out.'

Understandably the celebrations had gone on for a long time in Offaly after the Leinster title, but Healy and this team had their sights on an All-Ireland and, as a coach, he certainly wasn't going to be letting up on the players or even himself. He also made a point of constantly questioning and analysing his own performances.

'If you lost a match, the first place I'd look at was myself. Where did I go wrong? Was it in training or on the day? I analysed myself first and then would take it from there.'

His main concern for the next year was building on the win and to keep the momentum going. A second Leinster title in a row was duly collected when they beat Wexford by two points, and this time they made it through to their first All-Ireland final, where they were to face Galway, the reigning champions and the team that had knocked them out in the previous year's semi-final.

'I remember my main worry was if they were behind coming up to the end, they'd say, "Fuck it, we're beat." Every night, I'd say to them, "Look, Galway are playing a running game and we're playing it simple. With ten minutes to go, they'll be out on their feet. If we're within six points of them, we'll beat them."

'With eight minutes to go, we were six points down when we got a goal and that was the winning one. Pat Delaney said to me afterwards, "I saw the clock and I remember what you said. There was only six points in it, and I said fuck it, I'm going for this ball." It was amazing. But I didn't say that to them just the once, mind you; I said it every night, because you have to repeat things for it to really sink in.'

The players remembered all right, and what a way to show fortitude and belief, coming from behind and ultimately winning by three points. Incredibly, Offaly were the All-Ireland hurling champions. In just two seasons, a county that had no Leinster titles or All-Ireland appearances had won Leinster two years in a row and had just captured the Liam MacCarthy Cup.

Understandably, the county board wanted Diarmuid Healy to stay on, but he didn't know what he wanted to do. Had he taken them as far as he could?

'Then I said, "I'll stay on one condition. This is an opportunity to bring Offaly a step further. You've got to take charge of the underage. I want to see a minor All-Ireland within the next few years. Get the right people in charge and take it seriously. If you do that, I'll continue."

'"Okay", they said. "We'll do that." And in fairness they did.'

Five years later Offaly had won their first All-Ireland minor title and they were to capture three in a four-year period with Brian Whelehan, their future star, captaining them to their final minor success in 1989.

'Kevin Heffernan told me once, when I was involved with Dublin hurling, "The best way to promote Dublin hurling is you have to win a fucking All-Ireland" and that's it, everything else falls into place after that. You can have all the schemes you like, but unless your county gets that All-Ireland success it's next to impossible.'

Predictably, Kilkenny weren't going to take Offaly's success lying down and they recaptured Leinster for the next two years, although Offaly were to reach the provincial final both times. They had been a county with no history in Leinster, but now provincial finals were the very least of their ambitions and, by the 1984 season, in the GAA centennial year, they made their fifth Leinster final in a row, beating Wexford by a point. Cork were their opponents in that year's All-Ireland final, and it ended up being a demoralising ten-point defeat for Healy's team. Many thought this would be the final chapter in the team's remarkable run.

Healy decided to stay on and give it another shot but by

the start of 1985 he found he just couldn't motivate himself any more. The inner drive was missing.

'I was getting worried. "Jesus," I thought, "this is serious." Then one day I was going home at lunch and I saw this lad just passing by and he was reading a book. "What's the name of that?" I asked.

'"*The Psychology of Winning* by Denis Waitley," I was told.

'"Would you give me that when you're finished?" I asked.

'"You can have it now," he says. "I'm reading it for the second time."

'I took it home that night and read it. And because of that chance meeting and that book being put into my path, it was the cause of Offaly winning the 1985 All-Ireland.'

Sports psychology wasn't exactly in vogue in the early-to-mid-1980s, but that didn't stop Healy from lapping it up and in Waitley's book he found the answers for which he had been looking.

'This was about the psychology of winning, not only on the field but winning in life, generally. You don't just turn on the winning formula when you're going on the pitch. It's about everything in life, even from the time you get up in the morning. Compete, compete, compete.'

In his book, Waitley broke down the '10 Qualities of a Total Winner' as:

1. Positive Self-Expectancy – Life is a self-fulfilling prophecy.

2. Positive Self-Motivation – True winners dig deep.

3. Positive Self-Image – True winners are confident.

4. Positive Self-Direction – True winners know where they are going.

5. Positive Self-Control – Sacrificing immediate pleasure for long-term gain.

6. Positive Self-Discipline – The power to discipline and take control.

7. Positive Self-Esteem – Total winners are positive, powerful people.

8. Positive Self-Dimension – Total winners live in the present.

9. Positive Self-Awareness – Total winners are aware of their power.

10. Positive Action – Total winners are uplifting and motivating individuals.

'That's when I applied it to the Offaly players. I said to them, "Get up in the morning and when you're shaving, if it took you two minutes, try and make it one and a half minutes the next time." I was trying to get the whole psychology of competing into them, that, if you miss a ball, it's just another opportunity why you should win the next one. I'd be running around training and would be on a player's heels saying, "Come on! Another opportunity to win the next one!"

'I remember even in the run-up to the All-Ireland, I was going through Borris-in-Ossory and a guard pulled me over. I'm fucked, I thought, I must have been doing 100 in a thirty-mile zone. The guard stopped me and said, "Did you realise you're doing fifty-four in a thirty zone?"

'"Oh, thanks to be God," I said.

'"What do you mean?" he asked.

'"I thought I was doing 100." My reaction was so genuine he let me off. It's that compulsion – you're competing, competing, competing. That's the psychology of winning.'

Whether it was just chance that saw Healy getting his hands on the book, the serendipity of it all wasn't lost on him. With a changed message for the 1985 championship, the management and the team were refreshed and recharged. They beat Laois to retain Leinster and reached their third All-Ireland in five years, where once again they faced Galway. It was another close affair but, with the 'competing, competing, competing' mantra deeply embedded within that team, they atoned for the previous year's defeat and captured their county's second ever All-Ireland. It was a remarkable turnaround in just twelve months.

That was to be the last hurrah from Healy's Offaly team. He wanted to step down but was asked to stay on and he agreed to give it another year. Kilkenny were to get their revenge in the next year's Leinster final in 1986, handing out an eight-point defeat. It seemed as if things had come full circle from Offaly's first Leinster title under Healy those six years before. There was a need for change and for new players to come in as well, so he stepped down, bringing to an end his time of leading Offaly to historic, unprecedented and unparalleled success in their hurling history.

Most importantly, however, the culture and foundations for future success had been laid within the county; Healy's stress on providing a platform for the next generation of Offaly hurlers meant that this success wasn't just a flash in the pan. They went on to capture three Leinsters in a row from 1988 to 1990 and followed the 1980s up with two more All-Irelands in 1994 and 1998, the county becoming a major part of the 'revolution years' in hurling.

But, arguably, the real revolution came about in 1980, when Diarmuid Healy became Offaly's first ever outsider coach.

The history of failure Offaly had to overcome to make the breakthrough against Kilkenny in winning that first Leinster title, and beating the Cats for the first time in the championship, was arguably tougher than anything that the county faces in the twenty-first century, trying to narrow the gap to Kilkenny and Tipperary. But, Healy argues, the gap is not as big as people are making out. Instead, the problem still remains the same – that of mindset.

'I maintain now that teams up to this year that were going out to play Kilkenny had to be at least ten points better than Kilkenny to beat them. It was the same in Offaly, it was the same image of Kilkenny when I went up there. I remember a few years ago when Galway asked me to go up to talk to them and I was dumbfounded at their absolute lack of confidence.

'The thing is, the skill sets are not that different. But teams could be beating Kilkenny and then, going into the last ten minutes, it's a case of "Oh, we're beating Kilkenny" and suddenly, lads are dropping balls and panicking. They didn't know how to handle it. You have to teach people how to handle winning in the last ten minutes of games.'

The other reason for Kilkenny's continued success, in contrast to how the likes of Offaly have dropped away, is down to what's happening at club and underage level, and the quality of what they're doing, Healy believes. Counties have to improve how they're coaching at these levels.

'Hurling is probably the most skilful game in the world. It's also a very simple game and hurling played in a simple way can be most enjoyable to watch. However, although the ball can now travel faster and longer than ever before, players will only hit it twenty yards to each other.'

He can't understand why some of the skills are being lost or forgotten about, because in them he sees solutions for moving the ball at speed. Just to make a point, and annoyed with the possession-based game he was seeing develop, he got involved with his local club, Conahy Shamrocks, who were competing at the lower 'junior' level and hadn't won anything of note.

'We had a very young team, a very light team with no

physical strength in it at all. So I said, we'll play a simple game based on moving the ball quickly. You get the ball, immediately move, get rid of it. And the other players knew you were going to do that and so they're all moving too. Well, we won our county final, and we went on and won the club All-Ireland [in 2008] as well. That was the main reason I took on the job. I said feck this, I'm going to prove people wrong. That same team now, if you went with the way the coaching is going, wouldn't have got past the first round.'

For someone who preached a coaching mantra of positivity and of the glass being half full, when it comes to the development of the game he's more of a worrier, especially with regard to the fixtures at club level.

'You're coaching a club team, you start off in January or February and then you come up to May and you play the first or second round, and then nothing until September if your county's doing well. You can see the standard going down at club level because of that.'

He's still very passionate about the role of coaching and what kind of message and influence it can have on players on and off the pitch. It's coaching in the spiritual sense almost, helping the person in the wider scheme of things.

'There should be two outcomes if you're a good coach,' he explains. 'When you're finished, you should have a better hurler but also a better character. You can't have one without the other. You can't treat two people the same and some lad might be a bit more timid than another, but you have to bring him on. You never just criticise a lad and leave it at that. You must always have the pat on the shoulder as well.

'As manager you have to be everything to a player. A player has to be able to come to you and tell you the most intimate things about his life and trust you. I remember one player at Offaly who was playing badly came to me and said, "I'm having problems with the wife, I'm away from her every night."

'This was during the league and I said would a month off solve it? "It might," he said. "But sure, I don't want it known."

'"That's okay, take a month off." He came back then and everything was grand.

'When people might be telling me about such and such a player, I never asked what kind of hurler he was; my first reaction all the time was, what kind of character is he? I maintain if you have a good, strong character with average hurling ability, you can work on him. When under pressure at the top level, you have to have huge character to overcome it. In the dying seconds of an All-Ireland final, that's the best test of character ever. To win an All-Ireland, if you have players with character, they'll bring you over the edge.'

Offaly, despite having no history of doing that, were able to overcome it all. They won through the belief, skills and technique instilled by Healy. They overcame history, creating a new one instead. The legacy of Tommy Maher and the Gormanston courses helped the weaker counties rise up and proved that it could be done in the 1980s and beyond.

2

Faith:
JUSTIN McCARTHY

You must in all walks of life, have time for yourself and you must be able to see the beauty around you. You must see that to have a balance in your life.

When Justin McCarthy broke his leg in three places the week before the 1969 All-Ireland final, it was a cruel setback for the twenty-four-year-old from Rochestown, Co. Cork, as he was at the top of his game. Just three years earlier he had become the youngest ever Hurler of the Year and collected his first All-Ireland medal from midfield as Cork beat Kilkenny. He had collected a second Munster title in 1969 and seemed set to grace hurling's greatest stage once again as Cork prepared to face their old rivals, Kilkenny. As he rode as a pillion passenger on a motorbike in the days leading up to the final, his was the charmed life of the young hurling star, or so it seemed.

But then the motorbike went off the road and, as he lay there in agony, he knew his season was over. There was to be no final for him. A few days later he watched from a wheelchair as Kilkenny gained revenge over the Rebels for the 1966 final defeat.

How different it might have been, McCarthy pondered, if the accident had never happened and he had been on the pitch instead. A second All-Ireland medal might have been resting in his hand while the plaudits rained down.

But no, his journey instead was from the highs of hurling to the depths of despair. From having the world at your feet, your hurley strapped to the back as you rode on a motorbike around town, to the double pain of being stuck in a wheelchair and seeing Cork lose the All-Ireland.

After his accident, they had brought him to St Finbarr's Hospital in the ambulance but they could only help with the pain. The general surgeon was only in St Finbarr's every second night. He'd chosen a bad night to break his leg. When he arrived, the doctors took one look at his mangled leg, where the bone had come out through the side, and wouldn't touch it.

He was brought to the orthopaedic hospital in the city, but after three weeks he was still in desperate pain. They operated on him, then tried manipulating the bones back into place, but still he wasn't right. They took off the plaster and were hit by an awful smell. 'You've gangrene,' said the surgeon. 'I can't touch it for three weeks and you can't go back into plaster.'

They had to re-break the leg and put a plate with eight screws in. By Christmas he was still in hospital, allowed out only for a week before being finally released in February. It was to be another two years before they could take the plate out.

McCarthy never lost hope, though, never gave up: 'When I was in hospital I never believed that I wouldn't go back and play. I often said if I had to play in goal so I could be out playing again, I'd do that. Coming out of hospital there wasn't even any physiotherapy and I'd do my own physio to work myself back to fitness. It wasn't going to stop me. I never lost faith. What the accident did was it made me a better person.'

Cork won the Liam MacCarthy the following season as McCarthy watched from the sidelines, still not able to play. His path could have gone two ways after the accident: give up and give in, ditching his life's dream of playing for Cork, or instead, buckle down with even more determination and drive to make it back. If it had been the former, we might very well never have heard of Justin McCarthy, and his promising but brief hurling career would be a footnote in Cork GAA history.

What helped him through was his faith and belief that it all had happened for a reason. He was going to see it through no matter what. 'My father often used to say the darkest hours are before the dawn. You always remember there's going to be a dawn, always.'

He slowly got back playing with his club and by the end of 1971 he returned in the National League against Dublin.

Within a few months it was like he had never been away, even though in the middle of the league he had to have a final operation to remove the plate from his leg. Cork went on to win the National League and he was being lauded for his bravery in making it back.

By September 1972 Cork were again in the All-Ireland final and, by a twist of fate, just as in 1969, their opponents were Kilkenny. This time Justin McCarthy got to walk around in the parade and face off against the Cats in midfield. It was a classic final that swung one way and then the other.

With only thirteen minutes left, Cork were eight points ahead but, thanks to an inspired Eddie Keher, Kilkenny clawed their way back into it before finally running out seven-point winners. Kilkenny's victory was one of the greatest All-Ireland final comebacks. There was to be no fairytale return for McCarthy.

Cork lost their Munster title the following year and although they won the National League in 1974, their failure again in Munster that year signalled the end for McCarthy and he retired soon afterwards.

After what could have been a career-ending injury that cruelly struck him down in his prime, he had battled his way back for three seasons including that epic 1972 All-Ireland. He was left with just the one All-Ireland medal when it might have been more, but he was without recrimination or regret as he saw the strength he had mustered through those difficult months of his recovery and rehabilitation.

Not only that, but the enforced absence from the game also forced him into coaching and management. In 1970, still hungry for hurling and at the age of just twenty-five, he agreed to help coach the Antrim hurlers at the other end of the country. Coaching seemed to come naturally to him.

'I was always trying to help people, or a team, to develop. I wanted to enjoy the game and I want players to have success if they can. That's my philosophy all the time.'

As for the long journeys north to Antrim?

'Jesus, I liked the challenge! I used to go up there on weekends and I'd give them ideas to improve their game. When you don't have that much time, you're always trying to break things up fairly fast. When I was giving them ideas it all came down to very good practical training sessions. You must have that right and that's where a manager or a coach has to be able to look in and see what are they doing right and what are they doing wrong.

'You wanted to bring up their intensity as much as you could. To do that, you've to think fast. I often make the analogy: if you're driving from Rochestown to Douglas, you could say it was busy in Douglas today. Then you go up to Dublin and Jesus the cars are flying. Next you go over to New York and you think "I'll never cope here!" But of course you can cope after getting up to the speed of things. The speed of your mind and your reactions have to be good, you have to develop that and you have to develop your thinking and then your movements and so on.'

Not only was the journey a challenge, but the Troubles had also started in Northern Ireland by this time, with the beginning of the IRA bombing campaigns and the British Army on the streets. One Sunday when he was in Casement Park, Antrim's county grounds, fellas began fleeing, telling him to 'Get out fast – they're coming!' McCarthy joined them as they ran out of the stadium and across waste ground to hide out in a safer place.

Despite the challenges, however, McCarthy continued to coach the Antrim team. 'You could hear the bombs going off in Belfast. The thing was you'd do it for a cause and you're in a mind to help people out. That single-mindedness and determination to succeed was there always with me. I got that from my father. He was a hardy man and he was very determined. He was from West Cork and West Cork people are kind of stubborn and won't easily give in.'

Following his retirement from playing, there was a short stint as trainer to the Cork seniors before Clare's Fr Harry Bohan approached him to take over the Banner county in 1976. He was just thirty-one.

'Clare was a great experience. It was a long journey – five hours driving – and I said I'd think about it when they asked me. "We'd love to have you. I think you could really add to the team." Fr Bohan asked again. "I will," I said then. I was only young and the journey wasn't as much of a problem.

'I went there for one night and stayed for four years. I've a good feeling for people, it's something I know I have, and

I can sense whether they're tuned in or whether they want something badly enough. In Clare, I sensed the urgency with them. You must want something badly and then you have to be guided by somebody to do it.

'There mightn't be an awful lot wrong with a team, but they might just be lacking in areas where they just maybe don't believe in themselves or fall down a bit. They're also looking for that bit of a push, to generate guidance, enthusiasm, direction.

'I saw that in the attitude when I went up there my first day. Cusack Park [Clare's county ground] was being done up so we had to train out in Tulla, which was a long spin out. But there's a grand pitch there and for league matches it would be packed with people. The players were mad to do better and we did.'

Part of the reason for the crowds was the fact that Clare were going well in the league, reaching the final in 1976 only to lose to Kilkenny in a replay, before going on to win two league finals in a row under McCarthy, beating Kilkenny both times, with future manager Ger Loughnane on the Clare team during this time.

They were never able to follow up their league success in Munster, however, losing successive finals to Cork. Clare had developed a reputation of being the 'nearly men' in Munster. Whilst they may have won league titles, they would always fall short in their provincial competition.

It was the stigma of defeats like these that was to lead to Ger Loughnane's manic drive for Clare's successes in 1995 and 1997, although he had also learned from McCarthy's coaching techniques.

'And what were they?' I ask, and he takes out a notepad with pages of his ideas jotted down. It could be a manual for so many in the game to take on board.

'You must be able to take success and failure in your stride. That's important because it could get you down. But always have a winning mentality. Be self-motivated, and have huge energy. You must have a lot of energy. When people ask me, "What's the most important trait?" I always tell them that energy is very important.

'In a way you have to have multiple personalities to be a manager. You have to be a decision-maker and have a clear vision of what the team is capable of achieving. Have a cool head and be a clear thinker, yet be able to take advice from people around you. You must be fair, firm, diplomatic. You can't be above your station. You have to be able to take responsibility for yourself, the county, players, the whole lot.

'You have to be able to judge players' fitness and hurling abilities, as well as looking and seeing how the other team is going, you have to be looking into that too. There's such a thing as hurling fitness, which people don't always appreciate. People think players are very fit and they're flying, but I always ask, "How are they hurling? How is their hurling fitness?" Because when you're hurling it's not like running in straight lines. You must be able to stop and start, come and go in different directions, backwards and forwards. That's hurling fitness. If you get tired playing hurling, you're not that fit. That's very, very important.'

You must be able to judge players based on their energy and emotions, McCarthy believes, assessing a squad if they're flat or losing their appetite. It's about watching, reading and studying people.

'I study the game all the time because that's my hobby. I look at the team training and playing, and see different things straight away, from the way they're performing and what kind of standard they'd be. The good teams make less mistakes, they have a high level of intensity, of speed of movement, of anticipation, of accuracy. You'd see the energy out in the field and you'd know what level they're at. Whereas a lesser team is fumbling the ball, they're not as accurate, they're not as smooth.'

But energy can also be a reflection of one's ability to perform at a certain level under pressure, which may be reflective of mentality and mindset.

'In any game, no matter what it is, but especially hurling, as it's such a fast-moving game and there's so many sides to it, you have to be able to perfect as much as you can. Therefore you have to be able to have the confidence in yourself, in your skill, in your first touch. You must have the mental approach right and then you must be able to do things under pressure. You will never truly be able to play or train for a game entirely because the game is always going to be more intense, but you've to be conditioned as close as you can to the game in the training sessions that you have.'

Good decision-making, McCarthy believes, comes from the intensity of training (which is part of the reason for Kilkenny's success, McCarthy adds), but also through practice and programming. 'We're all programmed to a certain extent,' he says. 'From our first day in school we're being programmed and taught to think and learn in a certain way.'

For sport and hurling it should be no different, but the danger is when the creativity is stifled or lost in the process.

'With hurling being such a fast-moving game, you've split-second decisions to make and the only way that you can adjust to that is to have training sessions as close as you can to a game and then have a variety of different things that you have to do.

'You must have guidelines and fundamental things for players to know before a game but if you make it too complicated the good decision-making will be lost. Now, some players can adjust and they can see something during a game and I think sometimes with Kilkenny they have this mental telepathy that they can all get into sync together.

'I'd hate to be involved with a team that couldn't express themselves or play good hurling and certainly show off the skills of the game and still try and win. You don't have to be a genius to stop other teams winning, any fella can congest a team and bring back players and have three forwards only. I don't think you have to be a genius to do that. It's another way of playing but it's not the way that hurling should be played.

'I've a theory. If you have your work put in and you go

out and you're hurling well, you will run all day, play off the cuff and just go for it. If you make mistakes in hurling, you're afraid to run and will play safe. If you make mistakes on the ball, the first ball goes off your hurley, then the second ball you're thinking, "Will I go for that now or will I stay back? Have I or haven't I got it?" Then the ball is gone. You must be self-assured, which comes from belief and not being afraid.

'It's about the right technique and having the confidence to do it; it's keeping your eye on the ball, having that feeling, but so many players are afraid because they don't practise those things. It's a one-dimensional approach.'

Modern drills-based coaching – a common complaint echoed throughout the book by the managers – is a big problem, he says.

'Drills are over-stated in my book. I'm not a great believer in cones because there's no cones in a match. You must be able to think of distances yourself, so if you've guys thirty-five or forty yards apart, they must know the distance of their shot, how they can play a ball in and they must know from practice that the ball is going to go into a fella's hand or is going to go up to him. You can't be looking behind for the cones. Cones are too handy for fellas and they're too predictable. You've got to be able to manage space yourself.

'You also have to be able to read a game yourself. If I was playing centre back and I saw the half-backs at the other end of the field getting a ball, and you'd know from fellas that they could hit a ball fairly long, my instinct would tell me the minute that ball is hit, before it's even in the air, I'm covering back to make sure that I won't give too much space between the full-back and the half-back line and make sure I can pick up breaks if it does go in there. You do that automatically.

'If I was a centre forward and my half-back got the ball, sure I know straight away that they're going to hit it up the field, but if there's going to be a breeze coming off that, I can't be out too far. I've got to be watching, to come in and create, take up the space, watch the breaks and then take my chance. You have to give players the freedom but they must be able to read the game in the first place.'

After stepping down after four seasons with Clare, Justin McCarthy took over his native county in 1984 along with Rev. Michael O'Brien. This was the centenary year of the GAA and its historic significance was not lost on Cork hurling. It was an added incentive to aim for, especially as they had lost the previous two finals to Kilkenny.

Diarmuid Healy's management with Offaly in the early 1980s was shaking up the traditional hurling order at this time, especially in Leinster, and was proof that tactics and skills-based coaching could pay off. Tactics, positional changes and player switches were also being regularly employed by McCarthy and his peers. It wasn't about changing their style but creating the environment where the players could be confident going into a game, knowing they'd put the work in.

Their goals were set at the beginning of the season and the

centenary final in Thurles was large on their horizon. It was a chance to be remembered.

'"Your future is here now, lads," I told them at one of our first meetings in the Regional College as it was then [now called the Cork Institute of Technology] and which I still have the notes of. "You lost the finals in '82 and '83 but that's not going to happen any more. We have to change our whole mindset and we have to really commit here. The future of Cork hurling is inside in this room."

'I was looking to set the scene a good bit in advance so that they realised what they were aiming for and they'd never deviate from that, never lose focus. That's what a manager has to be. You have to be driven and ruthless. You can be the nicest fella going, but when you see something that you want badly, you can't have second thoughts. That's very, very important. You've got to be ruthless because you must do it for the team, the supporters, the county, county board and yourself, and you must be driven yourself to have that determination to do it.

'That must also be brought over onto the players. Sometimes players don't often see it, but when they look back they say, "Yeah, he drove us on there all right. There's no doubt he wanted something badly which we didn't realise."

'By nature, players always have doubts,' McCarthy concedes. 'I always say to players on the last meeting that we have before a game, don't ever listen to what anyone is saying [outside of the panel] because your mind must be strong.'

Confidence was generally never lacking for Cork hurlers and, sure enough, after the defeats in 1982 and 1983, they kept believing and won the centenary All-Ireland for the history books in 1984, beating Offaly 3–16 to 1–12.

Confidence and self-belief weren't an issue for the generation of Cork players almost twenty years later either. Justin McCarthy had just begun his six seasons managing Waterford when the Rebels went on strike in 2002 for better training conditions and input into player preparation.

'Well that's the other side of it,' says McCarthy. 'Sometimes they get too big for their boots and they think they don't need management but sure you all need managers. I mean they kind of took over. That was to the detriment of Cork hurling because these fellas got too high and mighty. The thing is I think that they went a bit overboard.'

One wonders how things would have ended up if McCarthy had been in charge but, as it was, he was observing the ructions in Cork GAA from a distance, albeit next door in Waterford.

Waterford were a bit like Clare in that they had a tendency to buckle and fail at the final hurdle. Their last Munster title had been in 1963 and since then they had been losers in five finals, the last one in 1998. But Waterford had always produced talented and exciting hurlers and had always promised so much. Could McCarthy make a difference?

His tenure began in July 2001. 'I remember the first night I met them. They had won nothing and they had had so many losses. I told them there were three trophies to be won next year – a Munster championship, a National League and an All-Ireland. "I want to see a cup coming into the town of Dungarvan and down into Waterford City. I want to see silverware being produced by this team," I told them. Of course they all looked up and they said, "We've heard that before and it didn't work out."

'"Well, we've to do a lot of things to get it right then," I replied.'

He brought his wife down to Dungarvan for his first match in charge, against Meath, and afterwards, although they won it easily, she said to him in the car, 'You'll win nothing with them. The Cashel team you trained in the '90s would beat them.'

'Don't you worry, we'll win all right,' he said. 'I'll tell you, I've plans for that team.'

'I needed to start on the basics. Their striking, I thought, wasn't good enough, while their discipline sometimes let them down. But there were also a few old chestnuts that were set in their ways. I only wanted fellas that are tuned in, I told them, and they probably thought I was a bit different. I don't drink, don't play golf, I'm only about the hurling.'

The training sessions started that winter out in Aglish in west Waterford. They were dirty nights with the wind and rain lashing in where the lights on the field were poor. The players were being taken out of their comfort zone.

'I remember one session the frost was glistening in the

field. The balls were getting so hard because they got wet and the frost had gotten into the sliotars. The fellas were saying, "Ah, Christ, this is ridiculous." I said, "Yeah, this is ridiculous. We have to do it, to put in the work. Think of the days when it isn't going to be so hard. Think ahead."

'There was a lot of managing in them but when you go in with any team, the first thing you must try and do is get to know their mindsets, their thinking, what they're capable of and try to improve on that.'

And it worked. The first season under McCarthy in 2002 they won Munster, beating Tipperary, the reigning All-Ireland champions, in the final to end a thirty-nine-year drought. For three years in a row they reached the Munster final, losing to Cork in the second year but gaining revenge in 2004. This was followed by another success in 2007.

Led by All Stars of the calibre of Eoin Kelly, Ken Mc-Grath, John Mullane, Paul Flynn and Dan Shanahan, the 2000s were to be a golden era for Waterford hurling. From 2002 to 2010 they reached six Munster finals, winning four, as well as a National League title in 2007 and an All-Ireland final appearance in 2008.

By that particular milestone, however, McCarthy had resigned, the players signalling they wanted a change. Despite their success in Munster, their failure to get to an All-Ireland final under his tenure was becoming a source of contention and they wanted a change of management to see if they could go further.

'Sometimes fellas are going off the ball,' says McCarthy. 'And they're not getting their place so they get a bit jealous and they'll get a bit narky and they don't want to see me there. I always tried to freshen things up as much as I could but it ended badly. It didn't work out for us [they lost the All-Ireland semi-final to Limerick in 2007, the last year of McCarthy's reign] but I knew there was a future there. "We'll get over this," I said, but of course it was a long weekend and they all got hot and bothered and they made a decision.

'They might have felt they wanted this, that and the other, but that wasn't going to give them what was really needed. It's like giving a child everything he wants. That's not going to make him a better person as he grows up and matures. I think what it comes down to at the end of the day is players listen to other counties and what they're doing, and they feel that if they're not doing that then they're not in the groove of doing it right and the management structure is wrong.

'If they could only stand back and say, "Do you know something, we got an awful lot out of that. There was an awful lot of sense spoken, there was an awful lot of direction given." They'll look back on that hopefully and see that ...'

Davy Fitzgerald took over in 2008 and brought them to an All-Ireland final, where they were trounced by twenty-three points by Kilkenny, and they haven't been back since. Since McCarthy left there's only been one more Munster title added, in 2010, and a somewhat familiar pattern has emerged with four Munster deciders now lost.

However, the county's performance in the 2016 All-Ireland semi-final, when they had Kilkenny on the ropes, along with the star performance of Austin Gleeson throughout the 2016 season, have given many Waterford hurling fans hope for the future.

Success under McCarthy has also helped bring on the Gleeson generation. With their fearless, risk-taking hurling, they could have been a joy to watch under McCarthy.

'I said to a man in 2006, "There'll be great players coming through Waterford eventually."

'"How do you mean?" he asked.

'"Because fellas have players to look at. They have heroes, they have a style of play to copy." We all had heroes growing up. We all copied fellas. We all wanted to be them. Kilkenny have them every day of the week, so they're reared on success. If you're reared on failure and if you're reared on doubts, you're going to play with doubt.'

After resigning from Waterford, McCarthy took charge of Limerick, but after reaching an All-Ireland semi-final in 2009, they lost heavily to Tipperary. A number of high-profile players were then dropped for the 2010 season due to differences between the management and players. The ousted players hit out publicly, criticising McCarthy, and although the county board voted to keep him on, that year was a struggle. After his team was knocked out in Munster and then in the qualifiers by Offaly, McCarthy resigned.

It was an ignominious end to a long and successful GAA

career. He had spent over three decades involved in coaching clubs and counties, bringing them All-Ireland, provincial and league success, but perhaps, in the end, the generational gap became too great and what younger players needed to hear were voices more in tune with newer methods and structures. But the principles remain the same and the dozens of notebooks that Justin McCarthy has are a record of his time dedicated to thinking about hurling, and are proof that the main principles behind skills, technique, people management, determination, focus and belief remain the same.

Much the same principles can be applied to one's working life as well. When McCarthy went for a sales job in his twenties with Top Oil he had no prior sales experience. 'You've never sold anything,' they said.

'I sold a lot of ideas to people playing hurling,' was his reply and he got the job.

'The Dutch people were in charge of the shipyard and they were hard taskmasters. You had to pull your weight then even though I was a young fella. They had a sign up in the workshop, I'll never forget it and I often quote it: "If you have five minutes to spare, don't spend it with somebody who hasn't." In other words, don't be idling around. I suppose it's like the fella in the field who's just stepping around – come on, there's always something to do.'

Indeed, his successes with Cork, Waterford and Limerick, as well as with Tipperary club side, Cashel King Cormacs – who had last reached the county final fifty years previously when McCarthy took over in the early 1990s, and who he then guided to a Munster club title within a year – are testament to the endurance of his coaching and management skills.

'I can enjoy hurling at any level and I've often trained junior sides to win championships just to see the joy and the adulation that they get.'

Enjoyment and pleasure from hurling is something he sees less of these days, however.

'It's a serious business and you can't dabble in this game. If you want to be successful, you've got to be able to specialise and you've got to have things right in order to do so. That'll take a lot of planning but it will also take people's time and it will always take people's ability. Have you the ability to bring this whole thing forward?

'In any walk of life the biggest single thing is managing your time. There's only twenty-four hours in a day. The man above didn't say, "Listen they're very busy down there, I think we'll put it up to thirty, and bring it up to eight days a week, because I think they're all under pressure." You've got to be able to manage your time. There's plenty of hours there but unless they're used properly, you're not going to be successful, in any walk of life.

'We're all being devoured by this monster we call progress. I've two brothers and a sister who went to America and going back over the years, they'd so many things on. They were working two jobs, working late, they'd this, that and the other. That was going back a long time but now we've had that here in the last twenty years and in the last ten years we've even got worse again. It's tightening and tightening and tightening.

'Life is totally complicated and congested. It's a mad rush. Then you're trying to bring in a game of hurling with more training and more responsibility and more exposure to the media and the whole lot. It's at breaking point. Realistically, it's at breaking point and it doesn't suit everyone.

'Players have to ask themselves, "Do I want to go to a certain level?" Or do you want to say, "Ah, I'm enjoying intermediate hurling and junior hurling, it's not too serious. I don't care. I've other things to do anyhow." There's so many other sports. Cork is a big sporting city. Athletics is big, basketball, soccer, rugby. Unless the guidance is there, even from the county board, and unless that respect is there for people, because I know people who are just sick of the way they've been treated and they say, "Forget it" – you must bring people with you.'

Priorities and balance are key. Justin McCarthy has been obsessed with hurling all his life but also appreciates and accepts its place in the wider scheme of things.

'You must, in all walks of life, have time for yourself and you must be able to see the beauty around you. You must see that to have a balance in your life.'

One of his other great passions is landscape photography, which is an extension of the great joy he gets in nature. It's an appreciation in a spiritual sense, in keeping with the Capuchins and St Francis of Assisi.

'There's an old saying and I often quote it to people: "Happy are those who see the beauty of the world around them. They will never grow old." I love the seasons. I've a lovely garden with the flowers, I have shrubs. I've a little patch in the back. I even have a pet fox. He comes into the house, jumps up onto the chair and I feed him.

'I love watching the stars at night and I love going out and watching sunsets, sunrises and reflections. I've five grand-children now and I bring them up the fields for a walk to see the corn growing and we catch the butterflies. "Do you hear that bird singing?" I'll ask them.

'"What was that?" they'll want to know.

'"That's a blackbird," I'll say.

'"And what's the other one?"

'"That's a robin. And see the starlings there? See how the swallows are going to be leaving shortly, they'll be going off to South Africa, they have a long journey ahead of them." You tell them a story and they're back to being a part of nature. It's important for your life to have that balance.

'An old friend of mine, he's eighty-six now and he rings me every fortnight to talk about the hurling and how I'm getting on. He tells me, "Justin, you must have a laugh every day and the day you don't is a day lost."

'I remember before we played Kilkenny in the All-Ireland in 1966. There was a very good priest in Rochestown, a Kilkenny man, Fr Roch. He taught me all about hurling. I said, "Father, would you say Mass for me before the match on Sunday?"

'He said, "I will, 'tis in my book, actually, but I won't say the Mass so that you beat Kilkenny. I'll say the Mass for you that it'll go well for you." Let's be honest, we're powerless people. Everybody has different religions and different beliefs, but the main thing is, faith is important.'

Mass and prayer are a daily habit for McCarthy. Faith provides strength, he believes, whether it's faith in a higher power or faith in life. He had faith in himself to keep going after the motorbike accident and he had faith that, somehow, things would work out.

They did, and while maybe it was not in the way he anticipated, it meant he found coaching and coaching found him.

3

Application:
CYRIL FARRELL

All you have to do is get your aims down, set your mind,
get working at it and I guarantee you will be successful.

When thinking of Galway hurling, most people probably remember the swashbuckling team in the mid-1980s that reached four All-Ireland finals in a row from 1985 to 1988, winning in the last two years captained by Conor Hayes.

They think of the maroon shirts lording it over the Croke Park turf and of Galway as always being a threat, of being good enough. Their success at All-Ireland club level has also probably something to do with the esteem that Galway hurling is held in, but at the same time, when you look down through the record books, while Galway hurling might have been there or thereabouts, most of the time it wasn't enough.

In Gaelic football, Mayo is the sorry barometer of perennially failing, of getting so close and not having enough to get over the line. After all, they last won the All-Ireland in 1951 and have lost eight All-Ireland finals since then. Some folk even talk of a curse having been placed on the county, reportedly when respects weren't paid to a funeral in Foxford by the 1951 winning team. Of the fifteen All-Ireland finals they have contested since the competition's inception, only three have been victories, giving them a win rate of just twenty per cent.

Yet Galway hurling can top even this. Until their All-Ireland win in 1980, they had competed in nine losing finals stretching back to their last win in 1923. Up to the present day, they've competed in twenty-three All-Ireland finals, winning just four of them. This gives them a win ratio of only seventeen per cent, though they should hope to improve this statistic in the coming years. Galway's league and Leinster titles in 2017 have them as most pundits favourites for All-Ireland success, if not in 2017 then certainly soon enough. Galway hurlers were the Mayo footballers of the time, yet in a few years in the 1980s they turned that losers label on its head and were lauded the length and breadth of the country.

What was to change so radically that saw them become a hurling county transformed? A young, thirty-year-old Galwegian teacher based in Dublin got involved and helped change the mindset of the undoubted talent that was there – of players who were aching to shake off the shackles of always losing. This combination brought them three titles in the 1980s. All told, Cyril Farrell has been responsible for seventy-five per cent of Galway's All-Ireland hurling titles.

'We were always the bridesmaid,' he admits. 'But I suppose the biggest thing in the late '70s was we had very good players there for a while but without ever winning.'

Farrell had never played at inter-county level, but just as with Diarmuid Healy, he was naturally drawn to coaching teams and soaking up as much information from all sports as he could.

'I was always kind of half-coaching at UCG,' he explains. 'If you were captain of a team, which I was for a year, the captain would be doing the training and you would have lads help, but I just liked doing it anyway.'

He was only twenty when he went to see the All Blacks, who were on tour, training in Munster. It opened his eyes, seeing them up close. The players were extremely fit but even back then their brilliance was in making and exploiting space on the pitch for themselves, opening up with the ball when the tackle was supposed to come in for them.

Farrell was picking up little nuggets of ideas and inspiration from all places, even while he was still playing in college. No surprise then that he was also to be found at Gormanston, listening to Kevin Heffernan talk about skills, space and movement.

'He would always say, make a move, and if the opposition sees you, you can counter it, but you dictate the pace, you make the move first. As a matter of fact, he said, if you want to, let them see you make the move.'

Farrell first became involved with the Galway set-up with

the U-21s in 1978, before coaching in his first senior All-Ireland final as a trainer on his predecessor Babs Keating's management team in 1979, aged just twenty-nine. As a trainer Farrell was introducing Galway hurlers of all ages to new ideas from across the sporting spectrum. A fast-paced possession game suited the Galway hurlers at the time.

His commitment to the cause was such that he drove up and down from Dublin on Tuesdays and Thursdays and back up for the weekend on a Saturday.

'When you were doing it you didn't feel it, but when you stopped doing it you said, "What in the name of God was I doing?" But I had been doing that for a few years and got used to it. I wouldn't mind, but it never dawned on us to change training from Thursday to Friday when I would be coming down anyway.'

He was juggling his teaching classes along with the time needed to travel from east to west three times a week, plus the actual training of the team. Monday nights were about preparing the English and history lessons for the Tuesday and Wednesday. On Tuesday he'd leave the school at 4.15 p.m. for the three-hour drive ('the journey was hell') through the likes of Kinnegad, Kilbeggan and Maynooth, arriving just in time for the 7.30 p.m. training session. Afterwards, there was just about time for tea and a chat and then he was back on the road east to be home after midnight, where he could grab some sleep before the next day's classes. Then he would do it all over again on a Thursday, before spending the weekend in Galway for training and matches, heading back to Dublin on Sunday evening to start the week all over again.

This had been his schedule already as trainer, so when the team lost the 1979 All-Ireland final (nine lost finals and counting since the sole victory in 1923) and he was proposed as manager, he jumped at the chance.

'I got a phone call the following morning and I accepted on the spot. Sure, I thought, it was a great opportunity. I wasn't thinking of the travel or time or anything like that. It was great to be young and to be able to do it.'

He's envious of those who can do such journeys on the motorway these days, but even a commitment like that with motorways and 120km speed limits would be a taxing and draining proposition. 'But you just do it,' he says, as he didn't know any different. Four years later he moved back west for good when a teaching job near home came up. For once he could actually chat, have a meal and spend time with the players and backroom team without having to worry about rushing off on a three-hour-plus journey back home.

When he accepted the offer to take over the Galway seniors, he did so without a moment's hesitation. He already knew the players, their talents, abilities and failings. Farrell might only have been thirty years of age himself, but he wasn't an unknown voice coming into the dressing room having to prove himself, especially as he didn't have the inter-county credentials.

'In '78 I was coaching and the whole crew would have

been there a good while without ever winning. I was training the team in '79 and when I became manager in '80, the biggest thing was to change the mindset, to say it was all right to win.

'It was a mental thing with those players as much as anything because they were a good strong group of hurlers, nearly getting there in '79 when we were in the final. The big thing was to change the mindset to win, to become winners.

'I think it was about confidence, really, making them believe. Getting into their heads that they were good enough. That when they put on a Galway jersey it makes them as good as anyone else, makes them as good as Tipp or Kilkenny. I always believed that when people in Connacht are good at something they would almost be apologising for it. It is our right to win as much as anyone.

'The skill sets would be the same and when you'd go into UCG, there would be hurlers from everywhere, from Galway, Tipp, Kilkenny or Cork and there would be no difference when they were playing in the same jersey. But the thing was when they were putting on the Kilkenny jersey or Cork, then they were different, they believed they were right up there.'

It's a refrain echoed by Anthony Daly when discussing his time playing with Clare in the 1990s before Ger Loughnane came along. An inferiority complex seemed to come over counties such as Galway or Clare, even though, hurling-wise, they were as good. The pain of losing finals can create that barrier, but as Cyril Farrell and so many other managers point out, so much of it is in the mind.

'We had a tradition of losing, so therefore we had to change their mindset. And we had this thing going round saying, "There's a curse on the team" and all this nonsense. I believe that a good manager is a psychologist in the sense that you have to know them yourself, one to one. You have to get to know each of the lads, how they tick, what's inside their head, and if you get to know how they perform, it's the same.

'When I took them on, I said, "Listen we are going to be the fittest team in Ireland and we're going to win." Now it wasn't as simple as that but it had to be a message they'd buy into and that's why they were doing the hard, physical training. This was the goal they had.'

Up to this point he felt the players and the team hadn't been suffering enough. Not just physically, but mentally. Losing wasn't hurting them the way it should. When they lost to Kilkenny in the 1979 All-Ireland, the players and staff were at a reception afterwards where they were all laughing and drinking together. Back in his flat that night Farrell vowed that if they were ever in a final again and they lost, 'They will be suffering, they will know what it's like to lose, they won't be happy and smiling.'

It wasn't, he felt, as if it didn't mean enough, but maybe they drowned it out in the aftermath. He wanted them to be hurting inside, to hurt so much that they would never let it happen again. It was also about imbuing them with the inner power to win. Rather than having to play well in all the matches, they had to be able to push themselves over the line when it really mattered and when they weren't playing well.

The long-term aim for the end of the season was set out on day one: winning the All-Ireland, and everything was geared towards that, including short-term defeats and sometimes having to take one step back to move two steps forwards.

'They understood that if we played a league match and got beaten out of the gate, it was because we were trying out things for later in the year. The whole thing was being built for the championship later on. We tried to win every game but it wasn't that we had to win every game.'

For Farrell, the way to play the game was to get the ball and lay it off accurately rather than hit it in hope.

'Play the percentages. I would try to get everyone moving together, which would have been unusual at the time because everyone would just play their positions.'

He met with the players in the dressing room in November to lay everything on the line and set out what he wanted to achieve for the coming season. With everybody crowded in he put the latch on the door and walked back to the table at the top of the room where he sat down and looked around him.

What did they want to achieve? Why did it not happen before? And what were they going to do to make sure they succeeded this time? It was all laid on the line and every player got the chance to speak and give some home truths. It was cathartic, a chance to leave behind the failings of the past and look ahead to the future with a fresh start.

'I was trying to get them to see that if we do the right things and if you follow me you can see we are going to do it, and that I believed it. They had to believe. I had to make them believe. The big thing was they hadn't won an All-Ireland medal. You might have an All Star but what did that mean? They still didn't have an All-Ireland. 1923 was a very long time and they were hungry for it. They were ready to listen and to do what was needed.'

Their first session was in January, playing UCG and then there was very physical training. It was tough, the weather was wet and cold and when they came in for their showers afterwards, the groundsman told them there was no more hot water.

'We have to go through stuff,' Farrell told the players. 'It's about suffering through it and you have to go into the showers now, cold water or not.'

The players looked at him, thinking he was crazy. Then they realised he was serious. They had to jump into the freezing water, whether they liked it or not. This was the way it was going to be. Were they prepared to pay the price, to suffer and believe?

'I was trying to get them to know that this year it was going to be different, there would be no comfort zone and no excuses.'

If you were late for the training, you paid the price. If you couldn't train, you couldn't play. If there was no hot water, you used the cold. No excuses, no second chance. It was the same for the season.

He also wanted players who had a strong presence, which he felt was missing. He wanted the goalie Michael Kennedy back but Michael said he couldn't do it, that his back was out. Farrell wouldn't take no for an answer and called around to his house face-to-face.

'He said, "I can't go back" and I just said, "Look, I have to have you." So he went away, spoke to the wife and then came back and turned out to have a great year for the county. I knew I needed him, I had no goalie like him. He was good if we got him right but he needed a lot of coaching and training.'

It was the only way to tackle any issues that arose – Farrell would go straight to the players' homes to talk to them.

'I always thought the best way to tackle anything, if you had a bit of a problem, if you wanted it thrashed out, was to go into his house. That's what I found useful. There's no barrier when you meet a person face to face.'

He also didn't have the luxury of great strength in depth with his panel, so whoever they had hurling had to hurl. You had to make yourself good enough, end of story. Farrell would travel all over the county looking at the players available to him and while some would only see a raw player, he would see something else, players who could do a job for him.

It didn't matter if you smoked like a trooper. As long as you were fit, could catch the ball in the air, take on men, lay it off and be strong, then you fitted into the Farrell game plan. It was a simple plan that suited the players in front of him. It was adapting according to the resources he had.

'I had one or two guys that could run with the ball very fast. If I had got them to hit it they were no good, their game was to carry and even if they had hit it, their game was carrying and laying off.'

By the time the championship started for Galway in July 1980 in the All-Ireland quarter-final against Kildare, who were the winners of the B championship, the hard work had been done. A ruthless victory led to them facing Offaly in the All-Ireland semi-final. It was a first meeting between the two counties in the championship and a first All-Ireland semi-final for the respective managers as well, with the two youthful coaches Cyril Farrell and Diarmuid Healy on the sidelines. The similarities between the two were remarkable: both in their early thirties, both in their first year in charge, both schooled in the coaching manual of skills and technique at Gormanston, and both looking to lead counties with little or no winning culture to new heights.

Healy's tenure was still in its early days and it was to be another year before his Offaly team made their own hurling history. In 1980 Farrell's Galway team, despite suspensions and injuries, pulled away in the second half with key goals from their impressive forward line of John Connolly, Noel Lane and Bernie Forde. 4–9 to 1–9 up with five minutes to go, Galway were in a commanding position, but the old failing of doubt crept in and Offaly stormed back with two goals and a point. There were only two points in it when the final whistle blew.

Galway had survived – just about – to reach their second successive All-Ireland. This time Limerick were their opponents. Galway got a dream start when Bernie Forde kicked the opening goal and it was to be a thrilling seventy minutes, with Limerick chasing Galway's early lead throughout. But in the end, Farrell's men won by three points, 2–15 to 3–9. Galway had their first All-Ireland hurling title since 1923 at the tenth time of trying. For the first time in fifty-seven years, Liam MacCarthy was going west over the Shannon to Galway.

In the aftermath, it was captain Joe Connolly's speech that was remembered, as he spoke in Irish and English, reaching out to Galway people not only in Ireland but around the world. 'People of Galway,' Connolly said passionately from the steps of the Hogan Stand. 'After fifty-seven years the All-Ireland title is back in Galway. It's wonderful to be from Galway on a day like today. There are people back in Galway with wonder in their hearts, but also we must remember [Galway] people in England, in America and around the world and maybe they are crying at this moment …'

'The whole place went mad,' laughs Farrell at the memory. 'It gave a great lift to the whole county and they could die happy to see Galway win an All-Ireland. Even the players themselves, they were trying so long, so just to win one, it was a relief.'

The team that won had undoubted talent, with the likes of Conor Hayes, John Connolly and Noel Lane, and the fact that they had been so close the year before meant Farrell hadn't been taking over an untried or untested outfit. But what was remarkable was that Farrell had been able to lift the hoodoo of half a century of defeat from the team and the county. He rightly focused on the mentality and mindset of the players and managed to cajole them into believing what he believed. It says much about the strength of character and force of will of the thirty-year-old manager that he was able to bring them so far.

One wonders, if they had fallen again in the 1980 final, whether that would have been it for that generation and whether later successes in 1987 and 1988 would have happened. Undoubtedly, the success over Limerick spurred on the next generation of talent coming through. Now that the seniors had proven that Galway was an All-Ireland-winning county, the mantle of success could come a bit easier. The minors now had All-Ireland heroes to look up to and seek to emulate.

They were to reach their third All-Ireland final in a row in 1981, where Diarmuid Healy's Offaly gained revenge for the defeat the previous year. Offaly had their first All-Ireland title and it seemed as if the young, schooled coaches were creating a new establishment in hurling, overturning the traditional heavyweights. But Cork and Kilkenny weren't long in returning to their dominant ways. The following year Kilkenny ousted Offaly from Leinster before going on to capture that year's All-Ireland over Cork.

That season was to be the last hurrah of Galway's All-Ireland winning team and it seemed as if the county would be in a state of transition for the next few years. But to ensure that the talent was still coming through, Cyril Farrell stepped aside and, in an unusual move at inter-county level, he took over the Galway minors instead. He saw the potential in the team and what it could mean for the future of Galway hurling.

The minors had been beaten in two consecutive All-Ireland finals in 1981 and 1982, so the talent was there. But, sure enough, in the 1983 season under Farrell, the county made it to their third final in a row and won it this time, beating Dublin to land their first ever minor All-Ireland – with the U-21s also capturing the All-Ireland in the same season.

A year later, Cyril Farrell was back living and working in Galway, and the crazy commutes between Dublin and Galway were at an end. Now he could concentrate wholeheartedly on hurling in the county off the back of the minor talent that was there and so was put back in charge of the seniors as they looked to win an All-Ireland again.

'Even if you win a minor or U-21 that doesn't mean you're going to make it up the step,' he explains. 'It's very hard to step up. If you were able to bring three or four minors up to senior level that would be very good. I was lucky in '85/'86 as I was able to dip into that pool of players which had big talent there.'

Future stars from that 1983 minor team included John Commins, Gerry McInerney, Pat Malone, Anthony Cunningham and Joe Cooney. As Farrell says when he brought them up to the seniors, 'They weren't as long to wean as the older guys.'

He was also more confident in himself and his own abilities. He knew how to do it, he had proven that to himself and the country.

'I was the same coach but I knew what I wanted to do. I was confident in that. It's not like you knew you were going to win but you would have been confident at the same time.'

A strong work ethic and belief about winning had been drilled into the players. Their 1983 minor victory, coming after two previous final defeats, was proof that they could do it and that strength of character would be needed in later years with the seniors.

Galway reached the All-Ireland finals of 1985 and 1986 but lost on both occasions. The danger now was that they were going to slip back into habits of old.

'In 1986 we lost in every final we played in,' explains Farrell. 'But then a small thing can change things for you. That year we lost a league final as well as an All-Ireland final and we were losing a lot of games. But they were a young team and in our team talks I would tell them, "I know it's tough but the common denominator is that we can also win them all; we will be a different team the next time around."'

The following year they won every final. Galway were the league and All-Ireland champions with pretty much the same group of players as the previous year.

'I'm not saying it was easy because it wasn't. Having reached the All-Ireland finals in '85, '86 and '87, we could have been losing three in a row and that's tough. But if you want to win and you're good enough, ninety-nine point nine per cent of the time the best team will win. The All-Irelands we lost we could have won, but the ones that we won we could have lost. It all balances itself out in the end. At least though, we were putting ourselves in the position.'

When success did come in 1987 and was then followed up again in 1988, Galway became the standard-bearers for hurling. Four finals in a row, and they had made sure it wasn't three or four defeats. They were reigning champions two years in a row.

With Conor Hayes leading the way on the pitch, Farrell wanted the players and the team to be about more than just good hurlers. He wanted them to be better people as well.

'If you're a good manager and if you want your team to be successful, then you will make them better and you will make the person a better person. I said to my team, "Nothing is beyond you." I would often say to them, "If you can put in as much effort into whatever job you like, anything is possible. If you want it, you can do it. All you have to do is get your aims down, set your mind, get working at it and I guarantee you will be successful."

'Now, you will be successful quicker in a business setting than you will on a sporting pitch because you won't have someone pitching the same field directly at you. When you get to the final and the other person is just as good as you, there is no guarantee. But in life if you want to succeed in whatever business, there's no barriers, it's all possible.'

Heffo's Dubs were a perfect example. That was a team built on determined characters, men such as Tony Hanahoe, Paddy Cullen, Kevin Moran and Gay O'Driscoll, who would have been successful no matter what sport or career they chose. What you bring to the pitch should be a reflection of what you do in your life off the pitch.

'I would be saying to fellas, we play hard on the pitch, as hard as we could, but off the pitch there's a standard which you have to have. You have to understand it, and it will open doors for you, and if you are good enough you can go through them.'

While Farrell was expert at maximising his resources, he argues the same is going on in the modern game with managers seeking to use the maligned and criticised 'sweeper system'. Unlike many vocal critics of modern management philosophies and systems, he refuses to criticise managers who set out with a strategy based on the players they have around them.

'You look at Davy Fitzgerald. He set up a [sweeper] strategy that he was going out with. Now, people mightn't like it, but it meant that the door was closed to the opposition. And don't forget, he has won an All-Ireland and a National League and they are two good titles. They will only think of that down the road. It's not that easy winning them.'

His biggest criticism of sweeper systems is that managers are misunderstanding their proper use.

'They can look terrible but guys don't realise that when the sweeper gets the ball, the opposition have an extra man up so you have to play two extra guys in midfield. You have to have about four in midfield – like a quarter-back in American football – so that when the sweeper gets it they can look up and get it into space. If the sweeper is good enough it creates chances and he can even run with the ball. The reality is, a lot of teams you see using it, especially at club, just don't have a clue. The sweeper is actually a quarter-back and lads don't understand that.'

The sweeper system, though, is something he expects to be developed more, especially as it's a way to stop leaking goals. However, until it becomes a way that starts winning All-Irelands two or three years in a row, then the more attacking and expansive way that Tipp and Kilkenny have been winning with will continue to be the system put up on a pedestal. But if things change, as they can so quickly in sport, who knows what way future All-Ireland hurling champions might be playing?

'If Waterford won two or three, would you have people copying their system? But you have to know what you're doing and why.'

While new hurling systems have been criticised for aping Gaelic football, the success of the Dublin footballers has brought back memories of Farrell's first encounters with the All Blacks when he was learning as much as he could. He sees many similarities between what the Dubs are doing and what the New Zealand rugby team does.

'They're doing exactly what the All Blacks did,' he says. 'Watch them. They're hitting the space when they go into the tackle. It's very smart and it's very good. The minute they turn over possession they have pace and they use that.'

As a manager you have to keep changing things, keep looking to advance your system of play. When Farrell went back to manage Galway for a short period from 1996 to 1998, he sought to introduce different elements to their game.

'We worked the hand-pass a lot – the reverse passing, breaking a tackle, giving a hand-pass. Instead of hitting it, look what you've done, you've got through a tackle and laid it off.'

No matter what, though, the special players are above and beyond any kind of systems, Farrell says.

'If you look at any of the top players, the Henry Shefflins or Joe Cooneys, they play on instinct. If you try and analyse and break it down, that's fine, but I guarantee you, the following day these players will have something different. Now instinct can be coached out of an ordinary player, I agree with that. But it won't be coached out of a top player. They just have something different.'

You have to be careful though with 'star players' at under-age, Farrell suggests. You often hear it said by managers that the leading players at minor level are wrapped up in a bubble which only harms their future prospects. Coming from someone who has managed minor and U-21 teams with such success, Farrell's words of warning must be heeded.

'It is only the first step on the ladder. A lot of the young lads now – and I know it's not right – but it can go to their heads a bit and next thing is they don't cope at all. It doesn't mean that because they're a minor they can just walk up to the senior level, it's a different ball game.'

Key to any team in Cyril Farrell's philosophy is having leaders from one to fifteen. 'They might be the best hurlers, but if they can't be leaders they are no good to me and I'm not doing my job.'

He lived for the job, for being on the sideline, imparting his vision and drive and making the players better for the team and themselves. Key to it all were those nights training, the players bringing the intensity to it all. It would make the three-hour drive worthwhile.

'The training nights would be very good and you would set them up in such a way that we would have very good matches in training. If it was going really well I might call the match off after thirty minutes, and if it was going very bad you'd call it off earlier. We'd have a break, have a talk, go back in.'

The type of player he wanted wasn't necessarily the star player. They could be with an ordinary club but, 'when you put them in an environment, put a jersey on them and get the team right, they're a different bunch.'

Farrell is an optimist when he looks to the future of the game. He sees better skill sets from the players – not necessarily faster, but certainly more skilful in different ways – he sees better diet, better fitness and recovery; and he sees a sport that is as popular as ever.

'I've never seen more young lads out hurling and they get more matches set up for them. They are competing against other sports but when you have a county like Tipperary, every young lad in Tipp wants to do hurling. That's why, with the likes of Galway, or like Clare lately, or Dublin, or Limerick, if you get a win it will carry you for a long time.'

The win that he oversaw with Galway in 1980 carried Galway into the successes of 1987 and 1988. It carried them beyond the legacy of 1923 and the nine final defeats. However, perhaps it also carried them into the 1990s with unreasonable expectations.

'The first time around there was nobody telling you how to win All-Irelands because nobody had won it,' Farrell says. In the 1990s, however, 'you had 30,000 or 40,000 who knew it all' and since then, there have only been four All-Ireland final appearances, all ending in defeat. It's going on thirty years since Galway were in their heyday, and even the talent of the likes of Joe Canning hasn't been able to push them past Kilkenny.

What they need, perhaps, is another, younger version of Cyril Farrell, someone to drive them on once more. But can they make the sacrifices needed without excuse? Can they believe again, ignore the past defeats and make their own history once more? Is there somebody willing to travel the lonely roads at night to make it happen?

4

Responsibility:
BABS KEATING

If you take responsibility for any team, and if you see no improvement whatsoever from the players, then somebody has to take responsibility for that.

While Cyril Farrell was able to reinvigorate a county that had stopped believing in themselves after so many defeats, one county that has never stopped believing in their own ability is Tipperary. One of the 'big three', along with Cork and Kilkenny, in numbers of All-Irelands won (thirty-six for Kilkenny, thirty for Cork and twenty-seven for Tipp), Tipperary has always regarded itself as being part of the hurling aristocracy.

Perhaps it was no coincidence that one of the managers from whom Cyril Farrell learned in his final year before becoming a manager was Tipperary man Babs Keating, who took Galway to the 1979 All-Ireland.

Keating starred on Tipperary hurling and football teams as a player and made his name as one of the best hurling forwards of his generation on the Tipperary team in the mid-to-late 1960s. He made his debut as a raw twenty-year-old in 1964, collecting Munster and All-Ireland titles in his first year before winning a second All-Ireland in 1971 and being named as Hurler of the Year.

This 1971 success was to be a twilight of sorts for Tipperary, however, as it was sixteen years before they captured another Munster title. For all their tradition and past success, it was remarkable how difficult it became to stop the rot once it set in. After the heyday of Jimmy Doyle and Tipperary hurling's domination in the 1960s, with four All-Ireland titles between 1961 and 1965, it was going to take somebody in the swaggering, outspoken mould to put Tipp back on top again after such a long drought.

That Tipp team of the 1960s was the county's greatest, and the reputation of the Premier County at the time was such that Kilkenny hadn't beaten them in the championship going back forty years to 1922. In 1962 the *Kilkenny People* was writing of Tipperary:

> *Every time the counties meet the 'Tipperary hoodoo' raises its ugly head and while we have been able to lower the colours of the Premier County in challenge contests, we have not succeeded in beating them in a league or championship match for more years than any Kilkenny supporter will want to remember ...*

If we could match Tipperary in determination, perhaps, we could go a long way of the road towards breaking the 'hoodoo'. We can match any county in hurling skill but while Tipperary never lack for earnestness, Kilkenny on the other hand occasionally show a tendency to lack that grim determination that is so characteristic of the Premier County and which has so often helped them to victory in face of the odds.

How quickly things change and history is forgotten.

Babs Keating, perhaps best remembered at the time for playing barefoot in the 1971 final because his boots were hurting, was the perfect candidate for bringing the glory days back to Tipperary hurling, as he understood the Tipp DNA.

He got his taste for coaching when Galway invited him on board soon after he finished playing in 1976. Management wasn't something he actively sought out but, as he says, 'I was up there as a name in the business, and I got the call from Galway out of the blue.'

He had been a leader on the pitch as a player, though, so it seemed a natural progression for him to continue on and bring that style of leadership into the dressing room as a manager.

'I would have been regarded as a leader when I won my last All-Ireland. I would have been regarded as a leader on the forward line with the guys down around me. I had two All-Irelands with a bunch of lads that had no All-Irelands, so naturally enough I think I was prepared to accept that role.'

Players taking responsibility, management taking responsibility and leadership – these were all key themes that

Keating was reared on in the Jimmy Doyle-led era of Tipp teams.

'In the previous teams I played in and previous All-Irelands I won, we were all leaders, we were a different group of players. Every player took responsibility and every player was prepared to voice their opinion.'

He is also keen to stress that it's not about management. Rather, coaching is the key.

'This word "manager" doesn't suit me,' he says. 'When you take management in the pure sense of it, we are not managing. The management of any county is done by the county secretary. He is the guy who organises everything. At the end of the day I am basically the coach, not the manager. I think that it's a misconception by a lot of people.'

The true role of a coach, as Keating sees it, is to maximise the potential of each individual within the team. If a team isn't performing and the players aren't improving, he places the blame squarely at the feet of the coach. That is their role.

'If you take responsibility for any team, and if you see no improvement whatsoever from the players, then somebody has to take responsibility for that. There has to be two areas that work hand in hand. First of all every player on the team has to be evaluated, knowing where they are at, and secondly, where are they going and what do they need to get there? Those are the key areas.'

Looking back on anyone's time in charge, these should be the criteria to be measured by, Keating believes, and he's not afraid to give himself and his selectors a mark of nine and a half out of ten when he considers their time with Tipp from late 1986 on.

Taking over a county that had seen barren times for such a long time, which contrasted so markedly with his success as a player, he focused on five main points: fitness, speed, stamina, style and skill.

'And those all deliver scores,' he says. 'Because at the end of the day if you have a player there and a goalpost there and a goalpost there, everything you do from goalkeeper to that other end of the field is about how many scores you get. Everything is geared towards that.'

With Keating's cupboard of Munster titles and All-Ireland medals, the players were willing and ready to listen.

'There was no situation that any player opposed us with that we hadn't an answer for, and we were consistent in our answers. There was never any deviation or any contradiction. We knew exactly the discipline that was required. So every night that we went training we had a discipline about us. It's the old story, a mistake is only a mistake when it is recognised as such. So I had no right to condemn anybody if we hadn't warned them in advance. We would have been very personal and very individual in that. Most importantly, the players bought into our policy.'

The carrot and stick approach was also important.

'You have to be cruel to be kind, let's be honest. You can't keep putting up with shit all the time. We all had to start on the first step of the ladder to get there and it was up to the management to maximise the potential within the squad.'

With talent from the likes of Nicky English or Pat Fox, it wasn't hard to recognise the potential that existed within that Tipperary squad when Babs Keating took over, along with Theo English and Donie Nealon as selectors. The onus and responsibility then lay on him to maximise it. This is a recurring theme when speaking to him about the modern game.

'I still can't accept that the Cork team I saw in 2016 could be so disastrous both in skill and with the combined play that was required. In the game where they were beaten against Wexford [in the All-Ireland round two qualifier on a scoreline of Wexford 0–23, Cork 1–17], I would say in the course of seventy minutes I could have picked out seventy or eighty mistakes that would be associated with junior hurlers.

'Okay, fine, not every county is blessed with the skill that [Tipperary's manager] has, but after the kind of investment that every county makes you would expect more.'

The players, though, also have a role and a responsibility in what they can bring to the table, he says.

'It's a two-way street too. I would like to think that from day one I would have put in place a system where the players were responsible for their own deeds. I would have always asked players to judge their performances after every game – everyone that played, no matter what game.

'We also instituted a system whereby the players them- selves would know about their level of fitness. I would have it on a graph for them from 1 January. Some players have an exaggerated sense of their own ability and I would like to think that we put in place a system whereby each player had a record of their own performances.

'I was in court once and somebody was up in front of the judge and he couldn't remember anything. The judge said, "I'll give you one bit of advice – the worst evidence is better than the best memory."'

The key from 1987 on was the fact that Keating had buy-in. The players and the county had been low for so long that they wanted to listen, to believe, and to do what was needed.

For the 1987 Munster championship final, Tipperary was to play Cork, a team aiming for an unprecedented six titles in a row, such was their dominance in the province and over Tipperary. After a pulsating draw in Thurles, the replay saw Tipp regain Munster with a nine-point win after a sixteen-year wait. It was an emphatic way to announce their return under Keating's management.

While they lost the All-Ireland semi-final to Galway later that year, the following year was to be somewhat more redemptive, as Cork were once again brushed aside in the Munster final. Keating's men reached the All-Ireland final this time – their first appearance since 1971 – against Cyril Farrell's Galway, who were the reigning champions and were making their fourth final in a row. They wouldn't be so easily cowed and in the end Tipp lost out by four points (1–15 to 0–14).

But the system was in place now for Babs Keating's players. They all knew what was expected of them, and most importantly, they saw that it was working. They were Munster champions two years running and were now pushing close to All-Ireland success. It had taken Galway until the third time of asking before they won the All-Ireland in 1987; all Tipp had to do was keep chipping away and surely success would follow.

They were committed and from 1 May 1989 there was no more drinking. But, for Keating, alcohol should only have been one small part of the sacrifice. It was to be all hands on deck to make the ultimate success happen. After all, that's how it was during his playing days.

'I grew up in an era where hard work was sacred. One day when I was training as a player, one senior passed a comment to me saying, "You are not fucking playing with my All-Ireland chances", and that was the approach by the players – they were so committed. When I took over, to be fair to a team that hadn't won for sixteen years, they were equally as positive. The only thing that they lacked was, having been down in Division 2 [the second tier in the National League] for a couple of years, they just couldn't grasp the idea that we could be winning an All-Ireland.'

How he got that message across was through constant communication and constant affirmation that they were good enough, that they could do it.

'It was about giving them that boost, constantly saying,

"Look, you are as good as anybody else out there." In fairness, it was easy enough to do because I was lucky with the bunch of players that we got in. The likes of Nicky English and Pat Fox, they were leaders. They proved it beyond hurling as well, as they've made it in business in their own right.'

The rivalry with Cork was also a big part of their motivation. When Tipp had faced Cork in Semple Stadium back in 1987 in the Munster hurling final, Tipp were not lacking in confidence.

'In the build-up, we knew that our players were improving and improving and playing the game the way it should have been played. We also had rules that we had back in the '60s that we applied to make our players a better squad.'

Keating had learned under the likes of iconic players such as Tony Wall and Jimmy Doyle in the 1960s and the lessons had remained with him. A style of play that maximised its effectiveness was key, he'd learned, ensuring that each strike was done with purpose.

'No player wearing a Tipperary jersey hits a ball when they have no reason for hitting it,' Wall told him.

'Now that takes a terrible concentration to apply that,' Keating says. 'That stuck with me forever more: no player strikes a ball unless he has a reason for striking it.'

Another rule was that, if you've got a strong full-forward line, everything should stem from getting the ball to those three players. Keating's full-forward line of Nicky English, Pat Fox and Cormac Bonnar were his key guys.

'So when we were training we were making the play for those guys and no player had the right or the authority to strike a ball unless there was a reason for it. So therefore there was no player taking a chance.'

Tactics and systems were nothing new either as, according to Keating, this was being done by that successful Tipp team back in the 1960s.

'The '60s team were regarded as the best team that played and it was generally accepted that our team in the '80s probably applied their approach of expansive forwards playing in an even better way. What has changed, and it has made a huge difference to the game now, is how far the ball is travelling. That has changed. Because in our case the ball didn't travel any more than eighty to eighty-five yards so you could certainly apply tactics.'

Keating's impact and influence on Tipperary hurling, while not quite mirroring the 1960s, certainly brought the glory days back and broke the Cork hegemony in Munster in the process.

They reached five Munster finals in a row from 1987 to 1991, the last time that had been achieved being exactly twenty years previously. Tipp were in their pomp again with the skill and flair of players like Nicky English proving that Tipp hurling hadn't lost any of its soul.

Despite the All-Ireland final defeat to Galway in 1988, Tipp were ready the following year and won an easy victory over surprise finalists Antrim by 4–24 to 3–9. Nicky English scored 2–12, breaking Kilkenny legend Eddie Keher's record points haul for an All-Ireland hurling final.

The team lost focus in 1990, losing to Cork in Munster (when Babs Keating's remark about Cork – that 'donkeys don't win derbies' – came back to bite him). But in 1991 they proved their greatness by capturing a second All-Ireland in three years with a four-point victory over Kilkenny.

It was to be the high point for Keating's managerial career and for this Tipp team, as they once again surrendered Munster to Cork the following year. Despite regaining Munster in 1993 and winning the league in 1994, Tipperary hurling was not to win another piece of major silverware for the rest of the decade. A four-point loss to Clare in the Munster quarter-final saw Keating step down in 1994, but his years in charge had brought All-Ireland success back to the Premier county amidst some hope that Tipperary's glory years were not just in the past.

Apart from the 1960s, Tipperary hurling had only ever blossomed sporadically, perhaps once a decade, and has never been able to truly build on its undoubted talent by creating a dynasty such as Kilkenny have done under Brian Cody.

Nicky English would manage Tipp to an All-Ireland ten years later, in 2001, and he admitted that it seemed to be the sum of the county's ambitions: shine brightly before quickly fizzing out. For a county of Tipperary's stature, self-belief and stated ambitions, it was a poor return and a poor reflection of the mentality and mindset within the county.

'When you get into a cycle like Tipp, when you only win a title once every ten years, it becomes a major event,' Nicky English has said in a previous interview for Joe.ie. 'Maybe when you break out of that cycle, players move on and get thinking about just winning the next game and not reflecting so much on the glory of winning an All-Ireland. That's really where you need to move it to.'

After English stepped down in 2002, Tipp were left in the wilderness for a few years – a predictable enough place in the aftermath of All-Ireland glory, it seemed. Cork were reasserting themselves in Munster while Waterford under Justin McCarthy were an emerging force. There were also rumours of problems in the Tipp camp as, in the autumn of 2005, Babs Keating's phone rang again. Would he come back and sort out the internal problems?

'When I was interviewed for the job the second time around, ninety-five per cent of the interview was around the word "discipline". Everybody else in Tipperary recognised there was a problem. I accepted the job, which I shouldn't have done, it was a mistake on my part.

'The players had an exaggerated view of their own ability and I had to tackle that discipline and make decisions that were right for Tipperary and we didn't shirk our responsibility in that. If you asked me to go over the same road again there is nothing I would change.

'But I regret having gone back. I don't regret the decisions I made when I made the commitment and I still don't believe we had enough players to tackle Kilkenny, who were at the top at the time.'

He points to players of the calibre of the Maher brothers who were coming through, but he still saw his time there as one to straighten things out and refocus the players. In the ten years he had been away from managing, players' attitudes and expectations had changed enormously – the Cork players strike in 2002 being just one example.

Coaching and communication had also moved on. Where the stick might have been previously used, now it was more about the carrot, getting player buy-in and proving to them that your approach was modern and up-to-date.

'In terms of attitude it was a completely different dressing room that I encountered in 2006 compared to the '90s. It was a reflection of the individuals that we had to cope with. Speak to Jim Gavin (Dublin's Gaelic football manager) about the Dublin squad and he'll say that you would enjoy their company. It was different with Tipperary at the time.

'The county board had warned me that there was a drink culture in the organisation in Tipperary and that it was rife. This was where I had my first confrontation, over drink.'

It was to be an uneasy two seasons without any success before Keating stepped down at the end of the 2007 season, his relations with many of the leading players – Brendan Cummins, Eoin Kelly and Lar Corbett in particular – having soured.

Keating has never been slow to voice his opinion and be

critical of players – a stint with Offaly in 1998 lasted just nine months when he compared the team to sheep running around in a heap and not listening to what he was saying – while the fallout from his second time with Tipp has since developed into a war of words with the county board and former players through newspaper columns and radio interviews. Keating dropped Cummins and Kelly in 2007 and in response Cummins wrote of a 'dysfunctional' team environment, and Corbett spoke of 'negativity'. In turn, Keating bemoaned the fact that he wasn't getting cooperation and couldn't get the players to listen to him.

The game and the players had moved on too far, it seemed, for Babs Keating to be able to reach out to them. It appeared to be another salutary lesson about being too far from the current generation to be able to lead. Sometimes the present doesn't want to know any more about the past.

However, Keating remains steadfast in his criticism of current hurling standards and believes the 1960s were a greater time for the game.

'I still think our skill level was far higher in the '60s than it is today. When I was growing up I hurled probably seven days a week. It's incredible the amount of players that I have seen in the last thirty years that haven't the competence to be able to play off both left and right, whereas there was no player that played on our team in the '60s that wouldn't have been strong on either side; it didn't make a difference to me whether I had to go left or right.

'If I applied the same to a jockey, if a jockey isn't as strong left or right, he's not really at it as a top jockey because he has to be able to cope with a right-hand or left-hand course. I knew I wasn't as strong on the left when I started out, but I deliberately used the left side all day in training and there were few players that I can think of that couldn't strike the ball on both sides. It just didn't apply in our time because we hurled seven nights of the week.'

However, he reiterates that it is the responsibility of management to ensure players are up to the standard needed.

'A player going out representing his county with ideas of winning an All-Ireland and who doesn't know how to play the ball, high or low, or fast or slow – he's not the complete player. So that's the responsibility of management to be able to say that all my players going out the door are equipped to deal with every situation that might arise.

'I see a lot of situations in the game today where I know players don't have a clue in hell how to deal with the situation. It's a skill in itself how to deal with a high ball, yet there's not too many players winning All-Irelands today that know exactly how to handle that dropping ball. The fast ball means that it's going quicker and it's breaking faster and it's a different game, but yet if you control the dropping ball you control the game.'

Concentration and preparation are also central to Keating's philosophy.

'No matter how good you are there's always a little bit

extra. There's always something you leave behind. Ninety-nine per cent concentration can represent 100 per cent failure. I brought in a Canadian sports psychologist in 2006 who spoke about a cyclist in the Tour de France who had cycled for maybe two-and-a-half hours on his own and coming to the line at the top of the Alps he put his hand up in the air to celebrate but that had done the damage and he lost in a split second. Or there was a race in Leopardstown where a young man jumped the last fence in front, galloped up to the line, put his hands up in the air and he was pipped at the post. So you have to apply for seventy minutes of hard work. As good as Tipperary were in 2016, I could pick out ten situations in their games where they lost their concentration and maybe could have got another five scores – all from lack of that concentration. Concentration and preparation are key.'

His answer to the defensive systems being increasingly employed by some coaches is that it won't work and coaches are fooling themselves if they believe otherwise. At least, so far, no county has won the Liam MacCarthy using that approach.

'The road to success goes back to your forwards. If you want to win, over seventy per cent of your scores must be scored by the three full-forwards, and I guarantee you that statistic will hold to the winning squads as long as All-Irelands are being played and won. If you decide to play with two full-forwards it's a contradiction and you'll soon find coaches will have to change their approach when they see it doesn't work. They're ultimately committing to failure.'

Looking to the future, and despite his spats with players and the county board, he sees an opportunity for this current Tipperary team and management to create something that hasn't been done since the 1960s. To create a lasting legacy and not just win the occasional All-Ireland.

'If Mick Ryan can hold the line in terms of discipline I think he has a better chance of applying them than any other Tipperary squad in the past. And with minor and underage players coming through, he has all the ingredients required to stay there. He has a team that should be young enough, because that team that won in 2016, there should be three or four All-Irelands in them.

'Those mistakes in the past around discipline, at least Mick Ryan has that knowledge and is equipped to cope with that. But I'll give no marks if he doesn't. The difference between what we did in the '60s and now, is that we were club men and I think you need that backbone there for the players. Your commitment to the guys you grew up with should be as great if not greater than even with the county team. And the thing about it is good healthy fellas aren't burdened with that much that they should abandon their responsibilities to their clubs.'

Words like responsibility aren't that in vogue any more and when Babs Keating speaks about hurling he does it with a strength of opinion and belief that is hard not to be met with either fervent agreement or disagreement. There is no middle ground. He engenders strong reactions from people who hear, in his language and criticisms, a throwback to the past. The glory days of the 1960s were over half a century ago, modern players will point out. What worked then will not work fifty years later. Sport and society have moved on. But he will argue that the principles should remain the same. Things like application, hard work, preparation, concentration.

He sees a softness in modern society and modern players that he can't relate to, yet sometimes it's not the manager's message that's the problem, but how it's being said. The days of players being given the hairdryer treatment are gone. Players are college-educated, have access to so much more knowledge than ever before and expect to be treated differently. For a generation of players who grew up in eras of 'do the work and just get on with it' and expected the same when they became managers, the world is a changed place. It worked up to the 1990s when players needed to be hardened and were hungry for success no matter what. Managers like Ger Loughnane and Babs Keating succeeded in their own way, in their own time. But they have found out we are now in a very different hurling landscape.

5

Instinct:
EAMONN CREGAN

The game is so flexible and should be understood that way.
Certain things can't be coached and come from just instinct.

Eamonn Cregan can't abide the hand-passing style of hurling that has been in vogue in recent years and was outraged when coaches tried to introduce the system to the Mary Immaculate College team he was managing in Limerick.

'My approach to the game is very simple,' he explains. 'You move the ball from A to B as fast as possible for the benefit of your own players at all times. A to B and get it up to the forwards quickly.'

'In Limerick we were playing to a system that we didn't understand. This system of short hand-passing is not our style and never has been our style. When Mary I played UL [University of Limerick] in the qualifier for the colleges' Fitzgibbon Cup, I just handed over the reins to Gavin O'Mahony [one of the other Mary I coaches at the time]. "You're the manager now," I told him. "I'm going over to the corner out of the way."'

But staying in the corner out of the way has never been Eamonn Cregan's style. A lifetime of hurling in Limerick and beyond as an All-Ireland winner, both as player and manager, means the game is never far from his thoughts, especially nowadays when he sees how it is changing, and not necessarily for the better.

Cregan was similar to Babs Keating, who was a rival in Munster in the 1960s and 1970s. Both were forwards with a good mix of flair and steel. It was an inner steel more than anything that drove Cregan, a self-belief, but also a belief about how and why the game should be played. What he saw at Mary I in recent years was a hand-passing philosophy that was anathema to what he knew.

'These guys decided that hand-passing was the game. At one stage the ball was in our defence and one of the players hand-passed it to another to another and so on for six passes to go from the full-back line to the full-forward line. I'm standing there at the other end of the pitch waiting and asking myself, when is the ball ever going to come in? The full-forward was standing static not knowing when the ball would be delivered. He couldn't make a run because he didn't know where the ball was going to go or when it was going to come.

'If you're a forward, you want the ball low, you want it

diagonally, you want it fast. With this short hand-passing game, the backs love it, they can close in and backs generally want a nice, closed game. I had words with the selectors and told them, "I don't want to play this game, it's ridiculous, it's taken six passes to get the ball up the field." So, we came to an agreement – eventually – that we did one hand-pass and we drove the ball up the field. And it worked.

'We did it against LIT [Limerick Institute of Technology] and UL and we beat them, although both games were touch and go. But this goes back to a manager's philosophy. What is it? What does it stand for?

'First of all you must have the players. They must have heart, they must have skill. They don't have to have the highest of skill but if they have the heart to fight for every ball and are willing to die for the player next to them then they will be considered.'

Winning the Fitzgibbon Cup with Mary I in 2016 for the first time in their history has to rank as one of Cregan's finest achievements in coaching and management, up there with All-Ireland success. All the more so as Mary I was never a traditional power in colleges hurling, having to compete with the size and reach of universities such as UL, DCU and IT Carlow.

'Mary I was traditionally for girls only and when that rule was lifted we had to drag fellas in wherever we could just to make a team. Over time it started to climb and only for Noreen Lynch [a lecturer in Physical Education at Mary I since 1972, who coordinated all the sport programmes within the college] there would be no GAA in Mary I. Slowly but surely I have seen it grow, and for the first time ever we were able to put in an intermediate team as well.

'Now, the budget that Mary I has for sport is small in comparison to the other colleges around here. They have basketball and soccer, and they now have a rugby team, they have hurling teams, they have three ladies Gaelic football teams, it's expanding the whole time. You have a lot of people coming through. Fellas are now coming to Mary I because they want to play Fitzgibbon. Teachers will all go out to their different schools later on but they will all remember Mary I. It's a different college, everybody knows everyone else.'

Mary I's 2016 success was to be historic in many ways. It was about more than just the players and management, it was about proving they could take on the big guns and win with their own philosophy and way of playing. And the manner of their victory over UL, in extra time, in Cregan's last involvement on the sideline after a lifetime in hurling, was especially memorable.

Facing the defending champions in the Fitzgibbon Cup final, in terms of size, facilities and budget, was akin to David versus Goliath. But, as the match ticked to full time, Mary I were in front by a point, before getting pegged back in the last minute. Extra time beckoned.

It ebbed and flowed, as Mary I went ahead and UL made it all square again. Cregan was as lively as ever on the sideline, pacing up and down the pitch, living every puck, score, free and hit. At one stage he even approached the referee, asking him, '"Excuse me, but is a player allowed to attack the hurley when his opponent is about to catch the ball?" He didn't answer me. So I said, "Okay, thanks very much" and I walked away.'

He needn't have worried about the ref, UL or anyone else for that matter, because two points in the eighty-eighth and ninetieth minutes sealed the historic victory for the college.

'All I saw was the keeper with his hands in the air, and it was just one of those moments that I will never forget. I couldn't believe that the same day as my wedding anniversary, the very same day thirty-four years ago, we won it. I was taking my wife, Ciara, out that night. It was incredible, it was just one of those days of – how could Mary Immaculate College win a Fitzgibbon? The after-effect for the college was huge because now it was on the map. I signed off from hurling then and said, "Grand now, that's it."'

It was a fitting way to sign off on his hurling career. Finishing in his home county of Limerick, making a stamp for the underdog, and doing so without compromising on a philosophy or vision for the game that he feels is being tampered with by modern coaching.

'It's not just a simple game of you go out and play; it's physicality, skills, game plans, all of these things and against Carlow [IT] in the quarter-finals we learned a valuable lesson about physicality and the intimidation that takes place. Some of the matches I've seen have been dour affairs and the tension and antics before the games unbelievable. Some of the things that went on – as well as the gamesmanship – makes me question the attitude of the teams and management because the players aren't doing it off their own bat.'

Eamonn Cregan was brought up with a respect for the game going back to the 1930s and the great Limerick team that his father, Ned, played in. It was a golden era for Limerick, with the hurlers reaching four All-Irelands in a row from 1933 to 1936 and winning two (in 1934 and 1936). His father's hurley from the 1934 All-Ireland final has pride of place in the Cregan home, and the wider, heavier base of the hurley hints at the type of game that was so popular in the past.

'It was all ground hurling, you see, you just hit the ball and it was really like shinty [the Scottish form of hurling, which is based on a ground hurling style]. They played ground hurling and they never scored points. There were very few points scored, it was all goals.'

Steeped in hurling, his father was a thinker about the game, offering him tips and advice along the way.

'I remember I was playing down Hanratty's Lane in Limerick City one day and as I was left-handed, I hit with my left side only. I got the ball, picked it up and I turned to my left. My father saw me. "You have no right side?" he asked. That's all he said and he walked away. Straight away I knew what he was talking about. So I developed my right side after that. Hanratty's Lane was where we would play and it was all about striking. We didn't realise it but we were learning how to hit the ball and it was so simple and enjoyable.'

After the heyday for Limerick in the 1930s, it was to be 1955 before they won another Munster title (there were four consecutive final defeats from 1944 to 1947). The team of 1955 that beat hotly tipped Clare were trained by Mick Mackey and became known as Mackey's Greyhounds, full of young, fast players playing at full tilt.

With an average age of just twenty-three, Clare were unprepared on that hot, sunny day for what they met. Just two years previously Limerick had been hammered by Clare by thirty points, but on this day Mackey's Greyhounds announced themselves to hurling with a ten-point win.

A lot of the players had come from CBS Sexton Street, where the style of ground hurling play developed through their fast pace and skills, and Eamonn Cregan and his generation were the next to evolve the game from these roots.

'I remember one Harty Cup [the hurling All-Ireland competition for secondary schools] game in 1964 where [CBS] Limerick's corner-back pulled on the ball, the right half-back pulled on it, then centre field pulled on the ball, the right half-forward pulled on the ball before the centre forward pulled and the ball went inches wide. Five players, five touches – bang-bang-bang-bang-bang – without the opposition touching it. It wouldn't happen today.'

Cregan was to make his championship debut a year later

against Waterford, when, he remembers, they had just four players training. The success of Mackey's Greyhounds was short-lived, but the generation it influenced would come to fruition over the next few years.

Cregan slogged with Limerick for six years in the championship before tasting a Munster final in 1971, which ended in a painful defeat to Tipperary. Two years later, however, they got their revenge. It was to be the first of four Munster finals in a row, of which they won the first two before losing to Cork in 1975 and 1976.

Importantly, though, the Munster-winning side of 1973 would also go on to capture the county's first All-Ireland since 1936, when they beat Kilkenny 1–21 to 1–14 with the help of Cregan, who was shunted back to defence to mark Kilkenny's danger man, Pat Delaney. The tactic worked and Cregan followed in his father's footsteps as an All-Ireland winner. He played on for another ten years, not retiring until he was thirty-eight.

It was in the early 1970s, still at the height of his playing days, that he first got involved in the coaching side of the game.

'Like my father, I was always thinking about the game. I first started coaching the U-12s in Claughaun in 1972 when I was twenty-seven. I remember my father coached us when we were minors – that's where we learned the proper swinging motion. Our left corner-back got the man of the match in the county final that day and they thought we had imported him in for the final because we had nobody of that calibre in the semi-final. But it was a simple exercise that my father showed us about swinging the hurley properly that had brought us on and it showed me the value real coaching could have on a team and on players.

'When it came to the Harty Cup we had Brother Burke and Jim Hennessy [as coaches] and they were unbelievable, they would rival Fr Tommy Maher in Kilkenny. If Brother Burke had been left in Limerick we'd be somewhere close to Kilkenny now. But they were transferred out of Limerick after a few years and were gone.'

Limerick's second heyday coincided with Eamonn Cregan's time as a player in the 1970s, but there hasn't been an All-Ireland won since 1973 and there have only been sporadic Munster victories as well.

Ironically, his greatest success as a manager came not during his two stints with his native county (1986–88 and 1997–2002), but with Offaly in the mid-1990s – although they were all learning experiences, he says.

'One of the things that I tried to get across to the players in Limerick in the '80s, which they didn't seem to take on board, was that we had met Tipperary in the Munster final of '71 and they had beaten us. We had met them three times prior to that and we had beaten them, and then we beat them in the league final in May and we met them then in the Munster final and they beat us by two points. In 1973 we beat them in the Munster final, but it was an accumulation of experience and being beaten and then coming back and winning. From

1973 to 1987 Tipperary had never beaten us in the Munster championship. Sixteen years.

'Our game was a simple game, it was the same type of game: we moved the ball, we didn't slow it down, we moved, moved; it was all fast ball. Okay people say it worked sometimes and it didn't work other times, that's fine, but I couldn't get across to the players in '88 that Tipperary are afraid of Limerick. And to this day there is something there and if we play it right we can beat them.'

Accumulation of experience is also important for coaches.

'You just don't become a good manager by going from a club and going straight into it, you learn your trade. And it's the same in hurling. Players must learn their trade. There are steps of ladders going up and you are always learning. But people seem to think that they come in and wave a wand and everything works out.'

When Cregan accepted the managerial job in 1992, Offaly hurling had fallen from the heights that it had reached under Diarmuid Healy in the 1980s, but the young talent coming through was promising much. The county had enjoyed minor-age success in the late 1980s and off the back of that group came a core of about nine players onto the senior team in the years afterwards, including Brian Whelehan.

First Cregan had to find some training cones though.

'When we went up to our first session we asked the officials, "Do you have any cones?"

'"What do you mean cones?" they asked.

'"You know, little triangular things?"'

'No, there was nothing, and so we had to use shovels and forks and spades to set out where we were to do the training. The players then did a warm-up and it lasted just six minutes. Six minutes! We had one fella that had been lapped twice in that time, even.

'But when they were hurling I could see why in games in the Leinster championship they were getting seventeen to eighteen points per game. They were the most natural hurling team. They would get the ball and bang, bang, bang, across it went. They knew each other inside out and you had John Troy, who was, in my opinion, one of the best hurlers I have come across.

'We did the physical with them to get them to a certain level and they were saying, "Why are we doing all this physical?"'

'"What happens if you are running for a ball and you don't get to it?" I asked them.

'I have a very simple philosophy about the game, but they were doing what I wanted them to do before I ever said anything to them. John Troy's job was to get the ball, run up and bang, keep moving, so the three half-backs [for the opposition team] are turning to run back. Once you get the defenders going backwards they are in trouble.

'So John kept moving it and his skill on the ball was just phenomenal, while the forwards knew it was coming. Players have to be intelligent as well, they can't be dumb or just robots.

They must be intelligent, they must be able to size up the game and they must be able to adapt to the changing situation.

'It's about instinct. And it happens in a split second. John Troy was brilliant at that. I remember John hitting a ball from inside the corner, right on the corner flag. He looked up and he got a ninety yard pass to the centre fielder over the far side who was all on his own, straight into his hand. You can't teach that, that's just there. He was the hub that the team moved around. You need players like that.'

By 1994 Offaly had regained Leinster and were to meet Limerick in the All-Ireland final. It was a game about which Cregan had very mixed feelings, as it had been so long since Limerick had won the Liam MacCarthy. But he was in the other dug-out now and that was just the way it was. He had a job to do to beat the opposition and unfortunately it was to be his own native county.

Offaly's victory by six points was bittersweet for Cregan.

'I will always have mixed feelings about it,' he admits, although there had been a first Munster title in thirteen years as consolation for his home county. The problem with Limerick, however, was that provincial success went to their heads, as he discovered when he took charge of the county from 1997, soon after their second Munster in three years.

'There was that atmosphere from that team, that they were a special lot. We had that thing in Limerick that if we win a Munster championship, they certainly went around and were opening this shop and that shop. It was to be a major problem for incoming management as we had to stop that because you are losing your focus from the start. How can you be playing in the Munster championship and the next week you are out opening a carnival somewhere? It had to stop. There has to be discipline there and the fellas in charge must handle it properly.'

While discipline was one issue he was trying to solve, so too was the thorny problem of the dual hurling and football player. While this issue doesn't affect Kilkenny or Kerry, for Limerick, where both codes are strong, it can prove a difficult nettle to grasp.

'Brian Cody has something that the rest of us don't have. He has thirty-five players that are good enough and he comes in and you are given your chance and if you don't make it, goodbye, whereas there would be a revolution here if you got rid of some players because Limerick is such a small place and the first man to be knocked is the manager.'

He came to loggerheads with his county board over this very issue in 2002, resigning when they wouldn't back him ruling out dual stars from the hurling panel. It was an ignominious end to his association with Limerick, but it did mean he was able to focus and help with Mary I's growth and development.

Cregan has also been an outspoken voice as he rails against what he sees as the imposition of a style of hurling that is foreign to Limerick. From the era of Mackey's Greyhounds to his own career built around fast-moving ball, he sees no merit in the hand-passing philosophy being imported into Limerick, and he places the blame firmly on the coaches' heads.

'When Dónal O'Grady [Cork's former All-Ireland winning manager] came to Limerick in 2010, he was one of those who imposed the short hand-passing game. For him, possession was nine-tenths of the law. That's well and good, but Dónal is a back. Backs defend, forwards attack. Cork had a team with the O'Connors on it and the short hand-passing game came from them and Newtownshandrum. They were playing this way since they were knee-high to grasshoppers and you can't deny it was very, very effective. But they played it at a very fast pace, everything was speed, speed, speed, whereas the current version of the hand-passing game is all slow, slow, slow.

'I'm worried about hurling going down the same route as Gaelic football, which started its hand-passing and possession with Thomond College in the 1970s. They were full-time athletes and terribly fit, so they could be running all over the field.

'However, these [modern] coaches are theorists. They aren't a Kevin Heffernan. He was a wonderful reader of the game but he also had the All-Ireland experience and a toughness about him that he was able to get players to do anything for him. He was someone who thought outside the box.'

Cregan sees in modern coaching a plan-based and systemic approach that doesn't allow for flexibility, instinct or reaction.

'Things don't always work as you plan it. You play to a

certain plan but if it breaks down you must be able to adapt and go to another plan. But theorists can't do that. It's the sameness of their thinking that creeps in. You have to be able to think of something else. It's about split-second thinking.

'In 1980 against Galway,' Cregan elaborates, 'Jimmy Carroll hit a long ball down the field and, as I came across for it, I realised the Galway goalkeeper kept the *bás* [base used to strike the ball] of his hurley on the right side, so all I thought was to get the ball and put it to his left. It just came into my mind in that split second and when the ball hopped I did that and it went in past the goalie. It looked planned but it wasn't; it was a reaction. If you're running theories or set plans you don't have things like that.

'In rugby, take Munster and Irish rugby legend Tony Ward as an example. A brilliant player but nobody knew what he was going to do and Tony didn't know what he was going to do until he actually got the ball either. But the sad thing is, a Tony Ward wouldn't make it nowadays, because he wouldn't be allowed play that way, he would have to conform to the system. And that's the way some people are putting the game of hurling. It's winning at all costs, keeping possession, and the style of game goes out the door. Now, there is a time and a place for it, but not all the time. It's knowing when to keep the ball in play and when to go for it.

'Even take Gaelic football and soccer, young fellas are all playing the same game. Coaches come up with a new "way" or system and everyone has to copy it. Take Jim McGuinness

– apart from the one All-Ireland success, when did they do it again? So much for the system and then there's the pontificating after the fact.'

But is he not then just a stick-in-the-mud, not adapting to the modern game and reality?

'That's not the reality,' he contests strongly. 'Because they're making it different. The modern coach, for instance, will tell you there's no room for ground hurling, but I can't understand that closed mind. Ground hurling is a basic skill of the game and is one of many skills. Coaches and managers don't understand it and they have to understand the game of hurling first. Fellas go in with preconceived ideas of how the game should be played.

'Take rugby; my son played it in Castletroy College and I saw one day he had a sheet of paper on the table with eight points on it. "What's that?" I asked him.

'"Oh, they're the commands," he said.

'"What do you mean?"

'"If one of those eight is called the forwards know what to do," he explained to me. Bloody hell, I thought.

'But hurling is different, hurling is not rugby. There is a basic core and part of it is that there are so many skills to the game and they must all be achieved. I always focused on the teaching of the skills. With my grandchildren now I'm teaching them the basics and showing them the most important skill of all: how to strike the ball. From your striking skills, your first touch, how you hold the hurley and the balance of the hurley, too many of our young fellas don't know the first thing about how to balance their hurleys or whoever is in charge of them doesn't understand the balance of a hurley. Ash is the timber and therefore there must be a slight give in it – it's the same with buildings and towers that have to have a slight give to allow for the wind. But a lot of our underage hurlers only have "boards". They go in wherever, pick one up and just go hurling with it. I used to be always touching up my hurleys, I'd shape them, lighten them with a sander just to get them a little bit lighter so there'd be a certain give down the handle of the hurley. But young fellas and their coaches don't know or understand this and yet in Kilkenny it's standard.'

Kilkenny is the standard in so much of modern hurling and Brian Cody, at the helm for so long, has also acted as ballast against the whims and fads of new coaching philosophies.

'They all go to a coaching meeting and all come up with the same ideas for how to coach the players and all teams are playing the same game,' says Cregan. 'I'm totally against that because Limerick should be playing a different game to what Clare, Galway, Waterford are playing. We're different hurlers, we have a different blood within us, we have a different game of hurling.

'The game is so flexible and should be understood that way. Certain things can't be coached and come from just instinct. If they knock vision out of players then it's a stereotyped game like American football, where the coach calls every play. You must have instinct, somebody who steps outside the box.'

Based on the current evolution of coaching and management he is fearful for where the game will be in ten years' time, despite the swashbuckling success of Tipp in 2016.

'If it keeps going the way it is going, it will be a sterile game and hurling is not a sterile game and can't afford to be. The hand-passing game will probably be even more dominant. You play the game for the players that you have. That's why it worked for Newtownshandrum and the O'Connor brothers.

'They were small, they were fast and skilful and the game suited them and suited Cork but that doesn't mean it suits other counties or other clubs. We've tried to play it here in Limerick and it's not us, it doesn't suit us. To me certain coaches are playing their game and making it a totally different game to what it is.

'I cannot understand a Limerick back running one hundred yards with the ball and then losing it. I often wonder do the people on the sideline actually understand what's supposed to happen when it all breaks down?

'If you look at the tactics at the moment, Kilkenny still play basically with six backs and so there's very little space there for forwards. They will play an orthodox game but when the ball is coming in [to their forwards] they will always have three players coming in at speed. Forwards have an instinct to score and they're gone like bullets, with a predatory instinct.

'Now backs are hand-passing the ball back to their goalkeeper and someday someone will handle it back to the goalie, it will be intercepted and it will be in the back of the net. Hurling is such a fast game and it's being slowed down.'

The expression in the game is now gone and they're all playing to the whims of the managers, Cregan believes.

'When we [Mary I] played LIT we knew what they were going to do and what they would be doing with and without the ball. We had to counteract the claustrophobia and crowding that was going on. It's a bit like watching kids and seeing them all chasing the one space and one area.

'It goes back to the coaches. Do they understand? Do they understand attacking? A lot of the managers today are goalkeepers or defenders. They have a defensive attitude.'

Players must also be able to think for themselves and react accordingly, Cregan believes. They shouldn't just be relying on the coach. The desire to improve also has to come from within.

'My father said to me a long time ago, "You put your hand up once to catch it, okay, that's fine, I'll let you do it once; I let you catch it twice that's a problem; I let you catch it three times, I take you off." Hurling is a simple game. Coaches complicate it. The players must think for himself and realise that if something is not working, then it should be changed.

'People say, "Ah, but you're a traditionalist" and I am a traditionalist, in the sense that players must know the basics and must have the basics. Hurling is basically a simple game – you defend, you drive the ball forward.'

His grandson Aaron is now playing the game, and knowing his grandfather played in an All-Ireland final means he is always pestering him about the game. They went into town after Christmas to get him a helmet, but not the fancy coloured ones. 'I want it black,' he said. 'I don't want any writing on the inside – exactly the same as your helmet.'

'The funny thing about Aaron, he and I didn't get on last year. I would have been saying things to him and he wouldn't do them, he would do his own thing. But we brought him into the store and I knew Mr Williams who was inside, and I said, "Aaron will tell you what he wants."

'I was outside then in the back and I was tipping out the hurleys and a lot of the hurleys are dead, they are flat, which is a problem when you are rising the ball as you can't get under it. So I showed my grandson and told him, "You have got to sharpen that." He came across a few days later and next thing he disappeared and went out to the garage and there he was with the plane in his hand, trying the same thing.'

For Cregan, seeing his grandson and his friends playing at U-10, it's about the importance of youth, the importance of the next generation coming through. Teaching them, making them think for themselves. He's had a lifetime of doing that in the game for county and, most recently, for Mary I. However, even though he's out of the game, he's not gone entirely. The Hanratty's Lane generation might have passed on, but he's still keeping those principles alive, still keeping it simple, still honing the instinct.

6

Character:
GER LOUGHNANE

I always believe if you have enough players of real character you can do anything with them.

As a player with Clare in the 1970s, Ger Loughnane had won league titles but never a Munster or an All-Ireland. Clare had competed in Munster finals in every decade (losing five out of the ten finals from 1972 to 1981), but their last provincial success had been in 1932.

Then, in 1995, Clare made history, capturing the Liam MacCarthy Cup after an eighty-one-year famine, but for Ger Loughnane, the Clare manager at the time, winning it just once wouldn't make this group of Clare players a great team. They had to do it again. And they had to beat Tipperary, then seen as the benchmark, along the way.

By 1997 Clare were in the unheralded situation of competing in their second All-Ireland final in three years and this time they faced Tipperary, one of the kings of the sport.

1997 was to be about more than a second All-Ireland for Loughnane. It was to be the culmination of his managerial philosophy. This involved giving players responsibility and choosing men of character, those who would stand up and never lie down. Integrity, backbone, character. These are the keywords in Ger Loughnane's hurling philosophy.

The first thirty-five minutes came and Tipperary were better than Clare all over the field. In tackles, blocks, hits and scores Clare were second best, and Tipperary appeared to be proving that Clare's 1995 success had been a one-off. As the referee blew his whistle for half-time, Clare were four points down and there seemed to be no way back. Clare's captain Anthony Daly and his teammates ran down the tunnel, heads down and expecting a bollocking.

Loughnane stood there and waited for them all to come into the dressing room. This was it, it was all coming down to these fifteen minutes in the dressing room.

'The first half was about desperately trying to keep our heads above water. We were in right trouble,' Loughnane explains. 'We were on the edge of a cliff. But, by Christ, we weren't going over it. Brian Lohan [Clare's full-back] led them that day. He got up and he put the hurley to their heads and he ordered them, just fucking ordered them, that this was what they had to do.

'To see the reaction from the players was incredible. I saw what was happening. I just stood behind the door and let it off. It was the culmination of everything, of giving them responsibility and then, when it mattered most, there it was, it came to the fore.'

It was there in front of his very eyes when it was needed most, as they faced down not only Tipperary but themselves in the bowels of Croke Park on that All-Ireland final day.

'You hear about dressing-room speeches but this wasn't even that. When Lohan spoke, he could speak in a voice so cutting it would go to the very marrow of you. It wasn't very loud but you knew it was totally genuine and brought out exactly what was needed; then everybody rowed in and they were like savages after that.'

God help anyone who stood in their way as the players ran out with intent and purpose steaming from them. It came from deep within that group, some of whom had never even merited appearances at minor or U-21 level for their county. Yet here they were, storming out onto the pitch, standing up for the county, the team and themselves.

'Liam Doyle got a great point at the start of the second half to get us going and I told him how important that was after the game. "Jesus," he said. "Sure I had to do something after what Lohan said to me at half-time." They had got back into their flow again. Whatever Lohan did, it burst the whole bubble and everyone just went out and did it.'

Doing it for themselves. This was the core of what Loughnane wanted. And not just at All-Ireland final time either. He traces the journey to Munster and All-Ireland success right back to when he started coaching the Shannon-based Wolfe Tones U-12s in the mid 1980s.

'There was a huge challenge at that time. Wolfe Tones were a new club and hadn't won anything yet at any level. But there was a great coaching system in the schools in Shannon and the danger was it wouldn't be carried on to club level. So I became very involved coaching the U-12s and U-14s, knowing the scene in the primary school and encouraging the kids and parents to get involved and get them down to the club.

'The biggest influence on me was I spent three years preparing to win one competition: the U-14 All-Ireland, the Féile na nGael. I took over the U-12s and we won the A championship. I said I'd spend two years with them, playing them at U-13 even though they were a year too young, all with the aim of getting ready to win the Féile – especially as it was coming to Clare the year they were U-14.

'All the things I later practised with Clare, I put into operation from then on. Maybe they weren't quite running up the hills in Crusheen, but we once trained nineteen days out of twenty – though it was all hurling, no running, all skills. Not alone were the parents supporting us, but people from Shannon started supporting the team because of the way they played. We won the county championship and reached the goal of winning the Féile in 1986 in our home county. That gave me a real taste for getting more involved at coaching.'

His key coaching tenets boiled down to three areas:

1. Playing the game faster than anyone else.

'All the hurling, all the coaching, all the practice, everything was done with a view to speeding up our game. It was the same philosophy of playing the game at a faster pace than anyone else was playing at the time.'

2. Total discipline.

'Players didn't give away silly frees and they kept the game open, no matter how much they were hassled by opposition, they were to pay no heed. They just put the ball down and played.'

3. Most important of all: character.

'It is a lot easier to shape a team at underage level as teenagers are more malleable, but it's also where I got the original belief in putting faith in the players on the field, even from a young age.'

Those underage players from over thirty years ago still stand out for Loughnane as he looks back on his formative coaching years.

'We had a player, Ciaran O'Neill, who was physically much stronger than the rest and was fully grown at that age. He was the captain at U-12 and U-14 and he had an amazing influence on the team. He had been given a central role not alone in playing but in organising things and telling the players when training was on. It wasn't done in a casual way; it was a calculated decision that the players would become central to taking responsibility.

'At national school, on those teams, I would get some of the players to give a talk at half-time and put the onus on them, telling them, "This is your team, these are your buddies and now is your time. Ye take responsibility." Even at U-12s they could do that. And Ciaran O'Neill would do that. He was a fellow of great character.

'He wasn't a brilliant hurler but he was a lad of great character. He would do everything he possibly could for the cause. It was fellas like that who I put in central roles in the team. It wasn't based on ability – far from it – it was based on fellas with real character. For they are the leaders. That's the first thing I look for. I always believe if you have enough players of real character you can do anything with them.

'Take Aidan O'Brien [the horse-racing trainer]. Did you ever hear him talking about how fast a horse can run over a furlong or two? No, you hear him talking about the horse's mentality. Transfer that to humans and it's character. They're the fellas you can rely on that will give you absolutely everything on the field.'

Such as Ollie Baker, the All-Ireland winner and All Star midfielder.

'When Ollie Baker was U-21 there was no way he would have been considered inter-county standard. When I saw Ollie playing U-21 against Cork he was marking Brian Corcoran and he could hardly hit the ball, but by God he made sure Corcoran didn't hit it either. He hassled him all over the field and I said to myself, that's a man I want on my team. I want a fella like that.

'Players' skill-levels, especially when they're young, can definitely be improved. When Ollie first came in we would put him in the centre with two hitting the ball at him and he would miss maybe three out of five shots, but a year later he was an absolutely central player. It's that kind of hunger and drive I always looked for in players, even from a young age.'

It's not about tactics or systems or stats, Loughnane believes. It's about the internal make-up of the players you're choosing to go do battle for you. But where does it come from? How do you define it? And can it be developed or is it innate? With modern sport increasingly ruled by science, numbers and the chalkboard, what place is there for something intangible and run by 'gut feeling'?

From *Moneyball* to *Blindside* and most recently, *The Undoing Project*, Michael Lewis has chronicled sport's and society's errors caused by ignoring or misinterpreting the stats. In *The Undoing Project* he chronicles how renowned experimental psychologists Daniel Kahneman and Amos Tversky revolutionised how we understand judgement and decision-making, disputing what our gut instinct tells us and proving that it is something that can easily be fooled and misled.

Ger Loughnane would strongly dispute their findings,

however, even if they are Nobel Laureates and Ivy League professors.

'It's hard to explain, you know it when you see it,' he argues.

This reliance on gut feeling is not so anachronistic that it doesn't have a place in modern sport. New Zealand rugby supports Loughnane's philosophy. One of the main things they look for in the schools is character and they develop the skills afterwards.

'If he has the character, the skills will be learnt,' emphasises Loughnane. 'It's definitely something that can be shaped, but if it's not there, it can't be instilled in them. If that attitude isn't there from the start, forget it. I see so many players who have the attitude but have been discarded for all the wrong reasons and it's terribly frustrating.

'The best fella I've seen in recent years is Liam Cahill, who is in charge of the Tipp minors. His philosophy on the type of players they want to develop is very good. He ran into trouble in Tipp about who was being picked because it wasn't necessarily the most skilful but the ones with the best attitude.

'The big problem with the "star" at U-12 and U-14 is he's indulged,' Loughnane points out. 'He doesn't work hard enough at his game and he doesn't have to because he can do enough to get by. But then, when he's older, he gets the shock coming up against lads who are hungrier, fitter, stronger than him. They work harder and the "star" can't cope. Instead, it should be about getting the right players into a system of preparation where it's all about attitude.

'Underage success doesn't matter. Who cares about who wins the minor or U-21 All-Ireland? It's about how many players are ready to step up to senior level. So few make the step up from minor – why? Because the wrong type of player is being identified and developed. If you can identify your crucial twenty players at U-14 or U-15, those who can really make it, and if half of those make it, you're flying. Character, it never changes.'

Michael O'Halloran, a winner of two All-Irelands for Clare in the full-back line alongside the Lohan brothers, is a case in point for Loughnane.

'When Mike first came onto the Clare team he didn't want to come on because he was barely getting on the Six-milebridge team. But I had seen him at an U-21 match and I liked the way he played. I persuaded him to come up to the U-21s when I was manager but Jamesie O'Connor destroyed him and he disappeared. I was thinking of him again and again when I was with the seniors so I asked him to come back and he did.

'I remember when we played against Antrim in the league it was to be his first ever game for his county and he was playing in his own ground in Sixmilebridge. He looked like a fish out of water and I was wondering what was wrong with him. The following Sunday though, we were playing Kerry in an Oireachtas Cup game and I put him on again. This time he was like a new man. Whatever clicked with him, something clicked inside with him and he never looked back after that. I knew from looking at him that he had the right stuff in him and he became indispensable to that team from then on.'

Loughnane believes this perceptiveness is one of the key traits required to be a successful manager.

'Have you the eye to see players of character from any age? I would have the eye, but some people can never see it. Players are being picked for the wrong reasons and they're being indulged. They win U-21, minor and next thing at twenty-three, twenty-four, twenty-five, where are they? They can't do the same things, they're being outmuscled and outfought and it all collapses around them.'

Softness is what Loughnane sees in his native county and beyond these days. Being soft and being indulged are probably the two greatest sins committed by players and coaches right around the country, he believes, with a few exceptions – notably Kilkenny, led by the man rightly regarded as the greatest manager of them all, Brian Cody. Not only is Loughnane one of his admirers, but he also knows Cody from their teaching-college days and says his man-management skills were marked out from that early time as well.

'Not alone is Brian Cody the greatest GAA manager of all time but he also compares to any manager in any sport. What he can get out of players is unique. Imagine to win two All-Irelands in a row [referring to Kilkenny's successes in 2014 and 2015] with that team in recent years! He could get the absolute maximum out of players with limited ability and he's an absolute master at that.'

Brian Cody has dominated the last fifteen years, Loughnane believes, because he has emphasised the qualities of character, effort and honesty. While others are going along with systems and buttering up players' egos, he's having none of that.

'Kilkenny were like Tiger Woods in his heyday. If golfers were facing Tiger on the last day of a Major they thought they were already playing for second place. The question is, though, how do you smash that aura? That was the big question for Tipp: had they it in them to smash the Kilkenny aura? In 2016 they did and now there are good signs they're going to kick on from that win as well.

'For a start, their celebrations didn't last very long. An awful lot of things have changed with Michael Ryan [the Tipperary manager], while the players from the U-21s from 2010 have matured really well. They are now going on the Kilkenny template of win an All-Ireland, celebrate for a while, but aim for the next one after that. What happened to that 2010 team was sinful, they just lost the run of themselves. The 2016 win, that was vital for them.'

Three Munster titles in four years and two All-Irelands in three years proved that Loughnane's Clare team kicked on after their initial breakthrough success in 1995. It was extra special, of course, given that it included a first Munster championship since 1932 and a first All-Ireland since 1914 for Clare.

'The belief wasn't really there for them to take it on until they made the breakthrough in Munster,' says Loughnane. 'Once they made the breakthrough, we didn't really feel under pressure. Always in big games, you'd see the players before and especially at half-time, they'd all come to the fore and they got into the habit of doing it.'

Winning Liam MacCarthy two months later, beating Offaly 1–13 to 2–8 in the final, was even more incredible, as the 1990s continued their remarkable run of All-Ireland victories by the so-called 'smaller counties'.

Perhaps, predictably enough, 1996 saw a drop-off in intensity and performance, and the Munster and All-Ireland titles were relinquished. But they had to do it once more if they were to prove themselves. It grated especially with Loughnane that people might question their 1995 success as they didn't have to face either of the big guns of Tipperary or Kilkenny along the way. But two years later they proved to everyone and to themselves that they truly deserved their place at the top table of hurling.

Clare didn't have to wait eighty-one years for another All-Ireland, but the surprising, unforeseen All-Ireland victory sixteen years later under Davy Fitzgerald in 2013 was unwelcome in many ways, says Loughnane.

'The success of Clare winning the All-Ireland was a very false thing. Now, don't get me wrong, it was a fantastic thing in bridging the gap between Anthony Daly's team and the present day in terms of the history of the game in Clare. But in terms of the development of the team it was a very bad thing, it was too much too soon.

'They were spoiled and indulged by managers and supporters. They hadn't beaten Tipperary, hadn't beaten Kilkenny; they had beaten a team [Cork] that were useless and the worst to come out of the county as has been shown. The final was a lovely open game and all that, but it was like a camogie match in terms of physicality. The challenge for them after winning it was to kick on and become a real team, but they haven't done that and the question now is will they ever?

'I look at Clare players and think they're like an U-21 team. Where are the men, the real men that stand up when you need them? Plenty of fellas shoot points from all angles and get headlines from gullible people, but how many of them would fit in with the Cody–Kilkenny mentality? How many would he have on his team? They just haven't made the step up to that level. It's a steeliness, a fucking hardness that's needed. I see it in Henry Shefflin, there's an iron steel that runs through him.'

That inner steel that Loughnane looks for is rarely seen nowadays, he believes, because of the type of youth coaching and set-up that has been introduced in Clare and elsewhere.

'The whole underage structure has changed completely. There is a softly-softly, molly-coddled, non-competitive element to it now. Young lads absolutely love competition and to win. Back in the National School, we would have hurling games in the yard and there were no helmets allowed on the tarmac. Now, I did have hurls with a rubber *bás* so they couldn't inflict serious damage on each other, but letting them out to play each other, it was savagery and they loved it.

'We used to have a seven-a-side league in the evenings and it would be all about "Flake the goalie! Kill him!", all that kind of stuff and they used to love it. They would spend all day getting ready for the evening game. Those lads have grown up and they still talk about those yard games in the pub to this day. But you can't even run in the yard now, you have to walk! This is rubbish stuff, it's all part of that softness that children are being reared in, that environment.

'If the character comes from within, then the toughness is hardened through savage competition on the training field amongst the players. Doing this at a level of hardness week in, week out, is what prepares them mentally and physically for the real battles to come.

'For the underage county players, they're either running or in the gym or doing these drills on the field going over and back, over and back. Drills are only fine if they're performed over a short time at a lightning pace. What made our [Clare] team was the absolute savagery of the [training] matches we had in Cusack Park. Fellas went down, we just kept going. They never went overboard, and neither Clare nor Kilkenny players would ever get injured in their own training matches.

'The more savage you go in training the better your discipline will be. Take rugby, when it's really hard and physical you get so used to it. If you hit a Kilkenny player a belt he would just ignore you. I remember when I was playing in the 1970s against Ger Henderson, Kilkenny's centre back, and our player pulled him as low as could be. Ger Henderson would have been entitled to have killed him. All he did was he caught him by the jersey, lifted him up and told him if he did that again he'd put him flying out into the stand. That's what real toughness is – being able to take it. And that's the greatness of Kilkenny, they can take whatever anybody gives them.

'Whereas now, with all the softness in training, you're going to carry this onto the field as well. For some of these Clare players it's nearly a non-contact sport. There's no hard tackles there at all and then if they met Kilkenny in Croke Park they wouldn't know what to do.

'The teams that have that toughness are the ones that are going to thrive and Cody has made the most out of the softness of others. When they come out, they make the opposition feel that there is a reason for their aura.'

It's not as if Loughnane has found the secret sauce to bring success wherever he goes. There were, after all, the two seasons at Galway from 2007 to 2008, which ended acrimoniously, without success and without Loughnane's promise of an All-Ireland.

'I went there with the idea that the players were desperate to win an All-Ireland. They weren't! Rivalries between themselves, the clubs, their own ego and profile was more important than winning for Galway. They had notions without anything to back them up. When you'd look around, you'd wonder where you'd find a Lohan or an O'Halloran? Did I see anyone like that in Galway? Absolutely not. The way players would perform for their clubs, showing the leadership and hunger for their clubs, they were not prepared to transfer that onto the county scene. It was very hard for anyone to understand unless you were there. You'd be coming home afterwards and you'd be shaking your head at some of the things they'd be saying to each other.

'When I went up there first, there was a big row in the county final and the following year the other players were talking about beating Portumna, "those Tipperary bastards". Players from their own county, this was! Sarsfields [a Ballinasloe-based club] were in the All-Ireland final before and I remember saying to a Galway county board official, "You'll be all going up to support them?" and he said, "We'll be going there to support who they're playing, not Sarsfields." That was the kind of attitude.'

After two years, there were no All-Ireland finals and only a league final appearance to show for Loughnane's time in charge, but he has no regrets.

'It was well worth trying. I'd have got a false impression if I'd only experienced the Clare years and think that the same characteristics and systems of preparation existed in another county. It was about seeing the importance of mentality. To go to another place and see their hurling mentality was completely enlightening for me.

'The club rivalry there is poisonous and brought to such

extremes; it's only the club and the club welfare that is the be all and end all, not being prepared to align yourself with other players from other clubs. If they were to take part in the Munster club championship it would do them a world of good and they wouldn't find it as easy to win club titles or be All-Ireland club champions.'

The difference when he was managing Clare was the player buy-in. They believed, and would do anything he asked of them. The likes of Anthony Daly and Brian Lohan, who had suffered years of pain up to 1995, were willing to do what Loughnane demanded of them and more. They wanted to win more than anything and if he could deliver for them then it didn't matter what it would take to get there.

'I have a notebook at home of the first training sessions when we took over. There were nine players at the first training session and none of those players started in the All-Ireland eleven months later. It wasn't all plain sailing, and certainly didn't start on a high. It started very, very low and was very gradual.'

It took off, though, because the players bought into it from the start. They were desperate to follow an approach that was different and which might lead to a different result. That was key. If they had all been new coming in, it would have been very hard, they wouldn't have had the willingness to suffer to achieve something at the end. They were prepared to go through anything and as a result they backed what Loughnane was doing.

'People underestimate when new people come in how difficult it can be to get players to follow you. When Pat Riley in the NBA [National Basketball Association] arrived at the Miami Heat, he met with the players and they told him, "You're our leader now. We're going to follow you." It's very hard to get that in the GAA because, when a new manager comes in, half the county is saying he's no good and the players are dithering and wondering who's going to last longest here? But if you have a group of players saying, "These are our leaders and we're going to follow you," it's a big deal. You had such big characters in Lohan and Daly but crucial to it was the lads we brought in also had the same character and mentality.

'Whenever anything wasn't going well you'd say to Anthony Daly, "You'd better have a chat amongst yourselves and sort it out." I wouldn't be involved at all. You can't expect players to take responsibility on the field if you don't give it to them off the field. That's one of the huge deficiencies in Davy Fitz's training. When he was manager of Clare, I was at a quarter-final behind the dugout when Conor Cleary hit a crazy ball in to the Clare forwards when there was nobody there. And what did he do? He went over to apologise to Davy in the dugout. What the hell?! That's the kind of control I'm talking about. Everything had to be controlled from the side as if he had the remote control. Spontaneity and effectiveness are lost as a result.'

Hurling has lost a lot through the devices and thinking of

modern coaches, Loughnane believes. From underage up to senior level he wonders about the efficacy of it all and where it's going.

'Early in the [2016] season, after the league finals and the first round in Munster between Clare and Waterford, I was desperately fearful. To all of my generation the Munster championship was everything, but its significance is being diluted year on year. Managers are only looking for teams to peak later in the championship. The last two Munsters in particular were terrible. The 2015 final was one of the worst I was ever at. At least in 2016 Tipp's victory demolished the Waterford sweeper system, but the other games were putrid.'

Loughnane has little time for the sweeper system used in recent years.

'I always considered the sweeper as straight out of the bluffers manual, going out with a defeatist attitude straight away thinking, "We don't want to be beaten by much." Going out with a negative attitude straight away in hurling is especially bad.'

However, he does accept that sport was always about getting your defence right first.

'Defence was a priority but this whole sweeper system was different, it was going out with a defeatist attitude. What was worse was all the defenders playing in a sweeper system lost the art of attacking the ball. They were losing the art of tackling and of winning their own ball. They're losing so much in the long run if coaches and players try to persist with it. The great thing though is no team has beaten Tipp or Kilkenny using the sweeper system and that is the only hope for hurling.

'Who's going to play with it next year? I don't think it will be as all-out or as bad as it was in the two league finals in 2016 – there were 7–8,000 less people in the replay when people should be bursting to see the game. It can't be as bad, that was the lowest point, crazy stuff. The nadir was seeing Tony Kelly, Clare's best score-getter, playing in his own half-back line, looking for a puck out from his own goalie. What saved the day were the [2016 All-Ireland] semis and the final. Waterford going hell bent and having the confidence to go for it. There's always a chance when you have the top four teams playing a certain way.'

Playing a certain way for Loughnane is about being true to the principles of the game, which have remained consistent. In Kilkenny, you can go back to Tommy Maher's time and on through to Brian Cody, when they preserved the same mentality and approach that has been sacrosanct down through all those decades.

'All the others who tried new stuff and methods, borrowing from soccer, rugby, the ten best ways to be a successful manager and all that kind of stuff. It wasn't successful. It's about the fundamentals, picking players of character who are genuine and would give it their best for the county. In all sport that is what works. Take soccer and Man Utd, plenty of talent and skill but where are the real men and leaders there?'

Modern-day coaches, he believes, are being brainwashed into conformity, which is ruining the development of teams.

'The next generation of coaches have to conform to the Google version of coaching to get their badges, all from the same place. Would Brian Cody qualify nowadays? It's a form of brainwashing and conformity and that's the big danger, but the teams that will triumph are the ones that break away from that. Liam Cahill [Tipperary minor manager] is the toughest one I've seen now and his thoughts and ideas on what the criteria are for players are ones to watch.'

The system of development squads is deeply flawed, he says, with characteristic self-confidence.

'Number one, the people in charge of them are not very qualified to identify talent and there is no co-ordination. Who is coaching the coaches? The coaches are being coached from the Croke Park manual, which is absolutely disastrous. The most important person in any county should be the person in charge of the underage development because the county must always be looking to the future. But the county board sees it as a diminution of their powers and they won't allow it to happen.

'There should be a group of three to five people that are the ones laying out the blueprint for the future – they can have divergent views but they are the ones who make decisions about who is put in charge of the team, what characteristics are being emphasised, who is running the development squads.

'You need a group looking at the development of players,

getting the mixture between skill and physique. It went so crazy in Clare that you couldn't be taller than five foot four or you couldn't play,' he jokes. 'They thought you could get a soccer Barcelona system into Clare hurling, it's crazy shit.

'You need brave players too,' Loughnane adds, 'because some look for the escape clause when it's not going well – blame the manager, blame the system, blame someone else. Maybe it's something bigger in society?

'The state is to blame, nobody is helping us. Are you helping yourself? What have you done for yourself? "We're victims" is a big aspect of it, but in sporting terms, great players won't blame anybody, they will only blame themselves. The great players take responsibility and when it matters most that's when they really assume responsibility.

'Take fellas like Conor Clancy [All-Ireland-winning forward under Loughnane]. He'd die for the cause. Never said a word but he'd put up his hand when it needed to be put up and no one else would. It came from players assuming responsibility and holding each other responsible. They were never blaming anyone else. [Brian] Lohan once said, "In every game we've gone out we always knew everything possible had been done for us in the preparation and it was up to us then when we went out." That was the whole philosophy.

'Dublin footballers take responsibility, Kilkenny hurlers take responsibility. Tipperary in 2016 did it. There was a new force there within them and it is only when that happens that you're going to be successful. The media create the illusion of the super manager and what he says at half-time and all of this, but it's nothing to do with it. As manager you create the pathways and structures but, as Lohan says, then it's up to the players to produce it.'

Like any great teacher, Ger Loughnane taught the lessons but then expected his pupils and players to stand on their own two feet and make it count. Whether it was the schoolyard leagues or the Wolfe Tones U-12s or the Clare hurlers on All-Ireland final day, he knew his work was done when, in a time of crisis, he could step back and observe as the pupils, without bidding, did as the master wanted. They stepped forward and showed their character.

7

Planning:
LIAM GRIFFIN

*We had our game plans but you fit the task to the player,
rather than make the player fit the system. You've got to
match the needs to the players.*

While Ger Loughnane attests that the secret to Clare's success was character, for Liam Griffin and Wexford – whose 1996 All-Ireland continued the dominance of the 'minnows' in the 1990s – resource management and game planning were key.

The brilliance of Griffin's management skills shone through as, in just two years in charge, he led the county to their first Leinster title in twenty-nine years, while Liam MacCarthy was also captured for only their sixth time and the first time since 1968. Furthermore, in the twenty years since he has stepped down, Wexford have only won the Leinster title twice and are yet to make it back to Croke Park on All-Ireland final day.

There were many similarities between Griffin and Lough-nane. There was the absolute passion for the game of hurling that precedes anything else, the drive to win and the pursuit of excellence; plus, they had the discipline and authority needed to instil winning habits and beliefs where before there were none. However, while Loughnane was perhaps someone of the old school in terms of thinking and playing, Griffin was a bit more exotic, more schooled in the wider influences of the sporting world.

While Griffin was, and is, steeped in Gaelic games, it was his family background in hotels and his commitment to the family business that ultimately influenced his management of teams and his understanding of how to win. The fact that he took that all the way to All-Ireland success proved it could work.

However, he is also quick to cut down any over-emphasis on the managers and believes this 'cult of the manager' is more a media bias than anything else.

'It started back in the '60s with Alf Ramsey [England's soccer World Cup-winning manager in 1966],' Griffin says. 'The press have to get an angle on the story and the manager is the one to hit. If he does very well, he's absolutely brilliant; if he does very badly, he's not any good. But that's not necessarily true, there's some great managers that have never achieved because the resources weren't good enough.

'I wouldn't like to underplay it, but I think there's a danger of overstating it, and there's a danger of being falsely modest as well. There's a balance to be struck at the management level. The balance is, you must have the resources, but you need good management as well.

'We're only resource managers at the end of the day. We're only as good as the resources we have. Brian Cody is a great manager but he's not going to bring Carlow or Laois to a final in hurling. That's not to take from the man, who is an absolutely great man and a genius to have held out for so long.

'I'm only trying to illustrate the point that resource management is all we're about, and if we don't have the actual resources to work with, we really can't achieve, and I just think, because of that, a manager's role is actually overstated.'

It's not a false modesty with which Griffin speaks either; it's a calculated, objective perspective that he brings to most things he puts his mind to. It's the right mix of being 100 per cent committed and passionate about the cause but at the same time being able to stand back and look at things as they are, not as one wishes them to be.

There's an easy parallel to be drawn between his experience and skill set in hotel management and managing hurling teams. Systems and structures came naturally to him. He studied hotel management in Shannon, then worked in Switzerland, the UK and Ireland in order to hone his expertise before taking over and running the Griffin Hotel Group. But for hurling teams, Griffin believes, one needs to go beyond systems and structures, beyond the theories and the learning.

'Yes, lots of the same principles apply, but you've got to

also put your own experience of playing the game, and your own experience of being involved with lads of a similar kind of a background or nature, to create an emotional connection with the lads that are there.'

Passion is the first and foremost requirement for Griffin but that then has to be coupled with something more.

'If you've got a passion, it becomes infectious, but if you can add that passion to structures and systems that are going to make the team work and keep it together, that's what's required.

'When you take over a team at the management level, you are the sum of all those parts, so you've all that knowledge that you have to distil down, transfer it to a team, but I think basically, that can become a bit infectious if it's authentic and you're genuine.'

Growing up in Rosslare he was the typical, sports-obsessed kid with a hurley always in his hand. 'Liam, for God's sake, would you leave that hurley out of your hand?' his mother would berate him.

His father was a garda and they lived in a row of terraced houses beside the barracks. He would go and play, hitting the sliotar against the barracks wall all day long. He found ways to test himself and improve his skill set. For example, there were certain nine-inch blocks in the middle of the wall that he had to hit.

'I'd hit one block and then I had to hit a different block and then hit another one. I never stopped until I got them all.

Diarmuid Healy, who brought success to Offaly hurling
in the 1980s when none existed before. © Ray McManus/SPORTSFILE

The Promised Land: Offaly players and supporters celebrate
a first ever All-Ireland title, beating Galway in 1981.
© Ray McManus/SPORTSFILE

Galway captain Joe Connolly lifts the Liam MacCarthy Cup after victory over Limerick in 1980. The 'curse' was ended after a fifty-seven-year wait.
© Ray McManus/SPORTSFILE

Cyril Farrell is congratulated by supporters after Galway's victory in 1988.
© Ray McManus/SPORTSFILE

Justin McCarthy, who brought Munster hurling titles back to Waterford once again. © Brendan Moran/SPORTSFILE

'I regret I went back.' Babs Keating watches the Tipperary team which failed to respond to his coaching mantra this time around.
© Brendan Moran/SPORTSFILE

Eamonn Cregan, whose success as a manager was about adapting to the players and not imposing a system first. © Diarmuid Greene/SPORTSFILE

Mary I's first-ever Fitzgibbon Cup success in 2016 was testament to Eamonn Cregan's hurling philosophy. © Eóin Noonan/SPORTSFILE

Ger Loughnane, who wanted players with character who would stand up and take responsibility. © Brendan Moran/SPORTSFILE

Liam Griffin attends to Martin Storey. Even down to the spare studs on the sideline, nothing was left to chance for Wexford's tilt at All-Ireland glory. © Ray McManus/SPORTSFILE

They had done it. Liam Griffin celebrates Wexford's 1996 All-Ireland success.
© David Maher/SPORTSFILE

The Facilitator: John Allen knew he had the trust of this group of Cork hurlers.
© Ray McManus/SPORTSFILE

Anthony Daly, who managed Dublin to Leinster and National League titles, but when will they achieve All-Ireland success? © Diarmuid Greene/SPORTSFILE

'We've always been hurling people.' Sambo McNaughton is in charge of Antrim hurling once more, but will the county be able to rise up again?
© Oliver McVeigh/SPORTSFILE

Eamon O'Shea speaks to Lar Corbett at the All-Ireland semi-final in 2015.
O'Shea brought a new way of thinking to Tipperary hurling.
© Piaras Ó Mídheach/SPORTSFILE

The Master, Brian Cody. But have other counties finally caught up with
what has been so deeply ingrained in Kilkenny for so long?
© Eóin Noonan/SPORTSFILE

It wasn't just hitting against the wall. It got to the stage that if I didn't hit them, I kept going until I cried. Just kept going.'

In the evening his father would send him down to the shop for the *Evening Press* so he could check out the late results of the horses. On his bike, soloing down the road, if the young Liam Griffin dropped the ball he picked it up and went back to the top of the hill to start again.

'I often came home bawling me eyes out because I had gone back ten times,' he says, and you can only imagine the reaction of the father waiting impatiently for his newspaper.

Worse was the time he had to put a bet on for his father and his father's friends in the bar. Outside the back door there was a gate and each time he passed by it he would hit a sliotar in the left and then the right corners.

'Out the door I went and buried this ball in the corner and missed it, so I went to bury it again. Eventually, I missed the race, and the horse won by 10-1. When I came back up, I said I was late with the bet and they went berserk. "What do you mean you were late? You were an hour before the bloody race!"'

Despite his hurling obsession, education and hard work were the mainstays of the Griffin household, which his parents both tried hard to drill into him. Foremost was his mother and, Griffin says, that was where he got a lot of his drive from.

'My mother was a really driven woman and she dragged us up by the coat-tails. My mother was the brains – anything you want to know? Ask your mother. Was my father a dogsbody because of it? No he wasn't; he was a strong, solid, big Irish man. He was a great man too, but he recognised early in life that this woman is fantastic, she's got the drive and the brains and I'm going to follow her. He was such a big man that he gladly followed her.'

His mother was the daughter of a farmer who had 100 acres of land. When she was just twelve her father died and her two brothers took over the running of the farm, while she went to secondary school in Kilkenny.

To earn some extra money Liam's grandmother began keeping guests in the farmhouse. This was his family's beginnings in hospitality and accommodation, which were to remain with them down through the generations.

When Liam was a kid, his father built a chalet on a bit of ground that was close to their house. They then took to moving out to this chalet during the summertime and letting out the rooms in the main house. Then, in the winters, his mother started a knit-work business. She started the garments, rising first thing in the morning before his father went to work, with the kids helping to pack them when they were finished.

Griffin's mother was determined her kids would also be educated and, as money was scarce, they tried to get county council scholarships for secondary school. Liam's older brother got one but Griffin the younger was 'too busy hurling' to get one himself.

He wasn't a completely lost cause, however, because his mother was constantly working, coming up with new ideas and saving money when she could to put them through secondary school. Then, when his father finished in the guards, his parents bought a hotel that was falling down, a decision which, unbeknownst to Liam, was to change his life forever. His sporting dreams, as a player, were about to end.

'I got loyalty from my mother, which means that when I meet her in Heaven, and please God I will, I'm going to blame her for me having to give up hurling because, for the simple reason, I felt such a loyalty to my parents for what they'd done for me that I went to Shannon to the hotel school to take up the hotel business.

'My father sat me down one day and said, "Liam, listen son, I know nothing about this business, and we're making a few bob, okay? Imagine what you would do if you learned it?"

'"Okay," I said. "I'll go to Shannon." So off I went to Shannon and the hotel school before going to Switzerland and England, but that really finished my playing career.

'I loved the hotel business, starting when I was twelve years of age with [making] the beds and seeing how well-loved my father was by everybody in the hotel bar. The bottom line was that it was a great example for me to have growing up and I had tremendous loyalty to them. I never wanted to let them down.'

He had won a Harty Cup and was playing underage for Wexford before hotel college in Shannon beckoned. Although he still played in Clare, his Wexford ambitions stalled and never came to pass.

He carried the regret of following that path for many years. Only in recent years has he been able to look back and not regret it. He still wonders, however, what might have been if he had kept playing, if he had remained in Wexford and focused on his ambition to play for the county team. Would he have been talking now about winning All-Ireland medals as a player? Success as a manager in later years couldn't compare, he says.

'Nothing can ever replace playing. No manager should ever get a medal for winning an All-Ireland. It can only be won on the field of play. If someone says managers should have a cup medal, I wouldn't have it. I don't want it; it's not right.

'As a player I never felt that I wasn't good enough to get to the very top if I wanted it, but I never achieved that, so there was always a longing left within me. And maybe the longing is to prove yourself.'

Whenever he did go to see Wexford play, he was appalled at how they were performing. He felt that a different way of thinking was needed for the team, one that perhaps his background could provide.

'I went in to watch Wexford playing so often and I thought, "This is ridiculous." Why am I saying it's ridiculous? Because I'm the sum of all the parts that have gone before and that starts to manifest itself, and you start to think differently.'

Brother Eugene Crowley was a big influence on Griffin's managerial style, as he learned from him as a teenager with

De La Salle in Waterford. 'The best trainer I ever saw in my life,' he says of his school's coach, who thought differently and was way ahead of his time with game plans and strategies.

But it was Crowley's ability to match players in the team for what they were good at and to make you feel important, that you had something to add, that he remembers him for most fondly.

'I always remember in one game him telling me, "Griff, I'm sending you to the far wing and if you get a break, take them all on. You're well able, we know you can do it; we need you today, you can do it." And when he asked me to do that, I felt, I'm going to do this because that's what he's expecting of me. It wasn't "You effing well do it" and all that kind of stuff. He never said anything like that.'

Thinking differently has always been part of Griffin's make-up. He played a lot of Gaelic football as well as hurling and was always looking beyond his immediate horizon to learn more. Griffin even admits that he'd prefer to be playing the present-day Gaelic football, seeing in it a more thoughtful, considered style of play.

The ending of his dream to be a senior Wexford hurler didn't stop his love and passion for sport in general, no matter where he was. As he travelled to Switzerland and England to continue on his career path, there was a void that needed to be filled. He did this by reading about and watching other sports, and when he came back to Ireland he did so with a more rounded sporting education as well.

The hotel business was occupying most of his time, but he was also involved in coaching underage teams in Wexford. There was still a longing there. He did a diploma in sports psychology. 'I wanted to learn stuff,' he says, and it was this desire for learning that led to him picking up Tudor Bompa's *The Theory and Methodology of Training*.

'I was never an academic, but I loved how he had references for everything that he was saying and that I could follow up on.'

Bompa's expertise on systems in training was just one part of what was coming out of Canada and its Coaching Association at the time, and so Griffin got in touch with them, hungry for more information.

'I didn't want to be getting stuff like Vince Lombardi quotes [Lombardi was the Green Bay Packers Super Bowl-winning coach in the 1960s, whose mantras about winning are much-quoted]. You know, "Winning isn't everything, it's the only thing". Yeah, right, okay. I looked at a lot of that stuff and it was just all clichés. I didn't want that.

'But in Canada they were producing a lot of stuff on sports psychology, on visualisation and strength training, and there were academic studies with verifiable data backing them up. So I got in touch and I started cross-referencing the books I was reading with other stuff, picking up more information and moving on to the next thing.'

By the time the manager's job for Wexford hurling was vacant at the end of the 1994 season, Griffin's name was part of the mix. But he was never a favourite for it until the leading names began to pull out. Almost by default, he was the last name left and was appointed as manager for the 1995 season.

As is often the case, it was about timing. Wexford had lost the previous three Leinster finals from 1992 to 1994. In 1993 they lost to Kilkenny in a replay after being four points up with six minutes to go. National League finals were also lost to Kilkenny, as well as an agonising one to Cork after two replays. For talents such as Martin Storey, Liam Dunne and Tom Dempsey, who had been hurling with the county since the 1980s, it seemed as if their careers might never see success.

Liam Griffin at least brought something different to the dressing room. What had they to lose? He brought in Niamh Fitzpatrick for psychology sessions, stats from John O'Leary, and Sean Collier for fitness.

It was a mixed bag of tricks and in the first season things didn't go well. Griffin was laying down the law, introducing a more strict regime, and when team captain Liam Dunne played a club match in advance of their Leinster semi-final to Offaly he was stripped of the captaincy. Wexford lost to the defending All-Ireland champions and afterwards there were rumours of discontent in the camp.

'Winning takes a while,' Griffin admits, 'but we came up with game plans for which there were no game plans being done. The game plan took a while to get it to happen, but one day it happened in an obscure match in Birr. We'd designed a plan to get a goal with a player put in the corner. The player was to go outfield and then was to come in at pace to receive the ball before burying it in the net. It wasn't as simple as that, but that was the idea, and once one of the plans works, you suddenly have players on board.'

1996 was also about making Wexford hard to beat and he has no problem with managers who use defence from which to build the foundations.

'We said, we have to be difficult to beat, so how are we going to do that? First thing is, don't foul. You stop fouling and you're difficult to beat. But it also means you have to attack the ball as a defender, and to be not afraid to attack it. We needed fellas that could attack the ball.'

They started from the bottom, breaking down the game, asking simple but probing questions. What is the game of hurling? What happens in this game? Then they moved it on, asking: why can't we be the best in Ireland at that? Once they broke it down, they realised there was no actual reason why they couldn't be the best at what they were doing.

'We may not be the best hurlers in Ireland,' they said, and Griffin pointed out to them that being the best hurlers in Ireland had nothing to do with it. Instead, there were a lot of things that make up this game that they could be the best at. For example, why couldn't they be the fittest hurlers in Ireland? Or the most committed? Or the most disciplined? He even introduced certain Eastern disciplines, like the Shaolin monks' principles that he'd read about, to show how disciplined and respectful you can be.

'In our game, you'd beat the shite out of a fellow and you'd beat up his father and mother if they came into the room as well. That was our aggressiveness, but that's uncontrolled aggression.

'Sports are about discipline, and with the Eastern disciplines, they're able to walk in, bow in front of their opponent, respect each other, go within an inch of killing each other, bow and walk out, and no one loses anything. One person wins, but the other person doesn't lose. They don't lose their self and more so, they don't lose their self-esteem. This stuff now where fellows are calling each other names and all of that, that's a load of nonsense. It's just disgusting, dirty, rotten stuff and it's no way to win.

'I'm not suggesting that we should be all a crowd of boys out there – it's a man's game – but my greatest satisfaction as the manager of the Wexford team was that we did it trying to do the right things.

'It wasn't any one thing,' says Griffin, looking back on that time. 'It was a combination of a lot of things. But one of the things that we tried to preach was calm, controlled aggression; you need aggression for our game, but it needs to be controlled. We had control of our minds and we had control of our aggressiveness as well, which was very necessary. We were conceding too many frees, you see. We weren't playing the ball. It wasn't that they contrived to do it; it was just that maybe they weren't either fit enough or mentally strong enough to try and just play the ball, which made them give away silly frees that didn't need to happen. You see that in every sport. You see it in rugby, you see all sorts of ridiculous things happen in sport. We tried not to do that, we tried to do it as best we could, which we felt would be the best way, and it worked for us.'

The team started winning again after that obscure game in Birr, and it became easier to get the players to believe in what was being done. Suddenly discontent became something that faded into the background. Whatever egos or personality clashes there might have been were being subsumed in the dressing room, as the players felt they were close, closer than they had ever been, to actual success.

For Griffin, it wasn't a case of walking in and setting down All-Ireland final day as the marker. They had to go deeper than that. It was about getting a group of players to work together to be the best they could possibly be and see where it would take them.

'I wanted the team to play the right way, because I'd watched Wexford play in the '70s and I got sick and tired listening to fellows coming home, complaining about this and complaining about that. I'm not trying to be unfair to some of the players back then, but I felt most of the times we were actually the authors of our own downfall.'

By the time of the 1996 championship, things were falling into place. They had reached the semi-final of the league, beating Offaly in the quarters – a satisfying turnaround from their defeat to them in the 1995 championship. They were even playing their keeper, Damien Fitzhenry, in the half-back line, so he would have a wider understanding and role for the championship.

Liam's brother, Pat, was a coach in England and he was able to get him a copy of the British hockey team training plan. Their strength and conditioning turned out to be about explosive power and speed, not just muscle building for the sake of it. Griffin talks about the essential focal points used by the British hockey team at the time in training. He felt there was a need to prioritise these points in Wexford's training in the lead-up to the championship. 'There's a triangle in training, which says S, S and E. Strength, speed and endurance. If you plot where you should be, you may certainly move around in that internal triangle, but you need to be over near speed and strength, having done the endurance, by the time you get to the competition stage.

'At the end of the day your team has to be fit for purpose, for the job that's to be done. Sometimes I would have to say to Sean Collier, "Sean, listen, I need more hurling. We've got this window to get something done, so can we work a system?" I wouldn't say, "You're the strength and conditioning coach, just go do it." What Sean was doing had to match the game that I wanted to play.'

In 1996 they faced Kilkenny in their opening match in Leinster and this time they were ready for them, winning by three points, before they saw off Dublin by six points. Offaly waited for them in the final.

As a young player, Griffin wouldn't have had much time for the rousing historically focused team talks revolving around Wexford's rich revolutionary past, such as 'Remember 1798 and Vinegar Hill!', but he knew this final was different. This was make or break for the team. They were heading to Croke Park for a fourth Leinster final in five years; he knew something extra was needed. He remembers walking the beach at St Helen's at 5 a.m. on the morning of the game, working his speech out in his head. The very survival of the game of hurling itself in Wexford was at stake, Griffin felt, and he needed the players to understand and appreciate that.

As their coach was about the cross the Wexford county border he got the driver to stop and pull in and he told the players to walk off.

'Breathe long and hard, we're walking out of Wexford,' he told them. 'And when we put our feet outside this county, you remember that when we put them back in here we'll be carrying that Leinster Cup.'

He spoke to them of tradition and its importance. A county of which they should be so proud – from Courtown to Gorey, Curracloe, Wexford, Rosslare, Fethard, Enniscorthy and Boolavogue.

'That's who we are and that's where we come from,' he said from the heart as the players walked in silence beside him. 'When they question the blood in our veins don't you ever forget that our county has a proud past and when other counties failed, ours was the only one of thirty-two counties where the people, your forefathers, rose and shook off the chains of bondage.

'Why should we fear Offaly or Kilkenny or any other Irish county? Nothing in our past suggests that we should. Look at your names. Great Wexford names. Think of all the memories that this county of ours holds for you. For many of the bones of our nearest and dearest lie buried in the clay beneath your feet. Like yours will, much sooner than you ever thought. This is our chance to make history. For which you will never be forgotten. You come from a fighting tradition and don't ever forget it.'

There wasn't a word spoken as the players listened to Griffin, thinking of their own past and their own demons that needed to be erased, so that a new history for Wexford hurling could be made.

That Leinster final day is one of his proudest moments as manager. It was when they hurled and truly expressed themselves against another great hurling team. And they won. Wexford captured their first Leinster title since 1977, beating Offaly 2–23 to 2–15 and ending an eight-final losing streak.

After promising so much in the early 1990s, Storey and co. were finally proving their worth. Tellingly, Wexford went from being three points up with five minutes to go to seeing out the game by eight points. They weren't letting their opponents back into the match like they had done with Kilkenny in 1993. There was a belief, a control and a determination there that hadn't existed before.

Into the All-Ireland semi-final for the first time in nearly thirty years, the other teams still standing were Antrim, Galway and Limerick. The opportunity was there for any of the teams, if they could take it.

Beating Offaly had shaken off the shackles of defeat. At long last they were winners and they believed in themselves. Game plans were being further tweaked with formations for frees and puck-outs being devised, while dummy runs and ways of opening up spaces were all being worked on. Rory McCarthy was the runner this time, coming in on goal from outfield.

'I said to Rory, "You could make forty runs, you could make twenty-five runs, you could make ten runs and get no score. That's the job. That's the job to be done. You just keep coming in. I want your defender non-stop always looking at his own goals, not looking at ours. Turn him around so that he's always coming in. He's coming in behind you, but you're so fast, you get in front of him and he'll never catch you, because you know what you're doing, because you're making the moves.'

'We had our game plans but you fit the task to the player, rather than make the player fit the system. You've got to match the needs to the players. Brother Eugene was doing it; I learned that from him.'

It worked a treat against Galway in the semi-final, with McCarthy grabbing the important goal to put them through to face Limerick in the All-Ireland final.

The final against Limerick was a 'perfect day', says Griffin.

The sun was splitting the heavens, Croke Park was heaving and 'Dancing at the Crossroads' was the Wexford theme of the summer.

But the best laid plans can also go awry. This occurred when Wexford went down to fourteen men with the sending off of Éamonn Scallan on the thirty-fourth minute. However, this only succeeded in concentrating the team's minds further and allowed Griffin and his selectors to showcase another dimension to their problem-solving abilities.

Griffin had mapped out all the myriad possibilities and probabilities that could happen and for which they had to prepare (including having spare studs on the sideline), and being down to fourteen men was one of those situations. As a result, they left Limerick's spare man be when in defence, but one of their forwards picked him up if they were a man over in attack.

Key to the game, though, was Tom Dempsey's goal in the twentieth minute, which put Wexford 1–3 to 0–5 ahead. It was a lead they were never to relinquish. Limerick only managed four points in the entire second half, two of which came in the last few minutes. Wexford's control throughout was total.

When the final whistle went, Liam Griffin's team had done it. They were All-Ireland champions. The ultimate test of planning and resource management had worked. Wexford were bringing Liam MacCarthy back for the first time since 1968.

Their two-point victory was, as Seán Moran wrote in *The Irish Times*, evidence of 'a team that bloomed in the realisation of its potential and the obsessive attention to detail and tactical mastery of manager Liam Griffin and his selectors.'

As the victorious team made its way back to the county there was a full moon shining down on them all the way. The villages and parishes were alive with celebration and, as they passed through Enniscorthy, Griffin allowed his thoughts to turn to Wexford's history – Vinegar Hill and 1798. This victory was about more than a game; this was about reclaiming Wexford.

It was also about people, place and family. His mother spent the game praying on her knees in a chapel in Rosslare, while his brother, Pat, in the UK couldn't stand the strain of the last fifteen minutes and was out pacing the street as Wexford's day in the sun arrived.

It was about the past, about memories of his Clare-born father, who was killed in a car that Liam was driving in 1971, and who would have been smiling down at having the best of it with Clare's win the year before and at Wexford doing it the following year.

It was about the influence of Brother Eugene, whose cajoling words helped spur on the young Griffin. Or the loyal son who gave up his own sporting career in order to push on with the family business.

As he met his mother on stage in Enniscorthy the next day, the past and the present all came rushing together. 1996 was an amalgam of more than a life; it was about families, mothers, fathers, sons and daughters whose lives were shared as part of this passion, this journey.

Twenty years on and Wexford haven't been back to Croke Park on All-Ireland final day. Liam Griffin hasn't been back as manager either, given that he stepped down after the win for business and family reasons. He is as outspoken and forthright as ever, however, about what Wexford needs to do to catch up and not let the sport slide away in his native county.

It's taken an outsider in the form of Davy Fitzgerald, with his appointment as Wexford manager in 2016, to come in and shake things up. Griffin makes it clear that he would have liked to see a local man in charge.

'I would have preferred someone from Wexford who had a similar passion to do the job, but we don't seem to have it, so then we can't really complain, can we? We cannot find a man of our own to come do the job, but Davy also needs us as much as we need Davy.'

Griffin believes in the talent that is coming through in Wexford (Wexford's U-21s won Leinster titles from 2013 to 2015) but better management of the county's playing resources is needed for them to succeed into the future.

'Someone needs to address this and say, "Lads, we've got to stop talking and start thinking a bit strategically here. What do we want? Do we want to be in Croke Park playing games or what?"'

They need someone of the calibre of Griffin, someone

with his management skills, to grasp the issue and deal effectively with it.

'I don't think if I went for election as a chairman [on the] county board I'd get twenty votes,' he says. 'Because I'd have to outline a vision and I wouldn't do the job unless I outlined a vision and people supported it. And if they didn't support the vision, I wouldn't do it then.'

His passion for hurling hasn't diminished one bit in the intervening years, while his own son, Niall, has followed his own passion – that of horses – representing Ireland at two Olympic games, including those held in Athens. Like his father, he too was an excellent underage hurler but decided to follow his other passion at a relatively young age. He did, however, go out on a high from the game.

It was the U-12s county final with Niall playing for his club, Rosslare, against Faythe Harriers. A bit like Atlético Madrid going up against Real Madrid, as Griffin puts it. A point down with three minutes to go, he called his son over to the sideline.

'Niall, if you're ever to hurl it's now, now is the time to do it,' Liam said. 'He left his position, which he'd never do, went out to the middle of the field, caught the ball, soloed through and struck it over the bar. A minute to go he caught the puck out, soloed it again and struck it over the bar as the final whistle blew.

'One of the selectors turned to me and says, "Where in the name of Jesus did that come from?"

'"Tony," I said. "I don't give a shit where it came from. We've beaten the Harriers in the county final, let's lap it up for a while!"

'Driving home in the car afterwards, Niall turned to me and said, "Dad, do you mind if I give up hurling?"

'"You've picked some day to say it!" I told him.

'"No Dad, it's interfering with the horses. I just love the horses," was his reply.

'"Niall, if that's what you want to do, son, by God, that's no problem, but that's a fine day to do it." And that was the last time he ever played a game of hurling.'

A passion for hurling is just one part of Liam Griffin's story. It's about having a passion for life and a passion for whatever it is you're doing, and then putting your heart and soul into it. It doesn't matter if it's hotels, hurling or horses, once you give it your all and plan for every eventuality.

8

Balance:
JOHN ALLEN

*I was facilitating them to be as good as they could be, but
I wasn't driving them on telling them this is the be all and
end all, I would never do that.*

You can easily imagine John Allen, bespectacled and quietly
spoken, in the classroom, mentoring and teaching kids about
the fundamentals of the world around them. He has that aura,
of a man centred, at peace with himself and his place in the
world. Not one for shouting or raising his voice, you'd imagine; more one to command respect through carefully chosen words. It is the same when you meet him over coffee and
question him on hurling, management and what it all means.

John Allen bucks the trend and the stereotype of the
obsessed hurling man. He's interested in a lot more besides
and could take or leave many aspects of sport and inter-county
management. For journalists, he's a study – not in indifference

but in stoicism and acceptance, his insights fascinating in any walk of life, not just in a sporting context. He's someone you want to know more about and someone with whom you can end up spending more time talking about everything but hurling. Music, especially, is Allen's first real love.

'The only thing now that would make the hairs stand on the back of my neck is something to do with music, and probably always has been. Somewhere inside of me there is a real love and appreciation of music. When I hear a really good rendition of some song, or a great band playing, a great choral piece, a great jazz piece, the hair might stand on the back of my neck. But that very rarely happens.'

He comes from the village of Aghabullogue, Co. Cork, where his father was a bus driver and his mother ran the pub. They lived across from the school and the school field, where John would puck about with his uncle Donal. The GAA was the heart and soul of the parish and of the conversations in the bar every night. The main focus for John, however, was learning to play guitar and buying records and music magazines. Music was always there.

'With the music I wasn't as good as I would like to have been. I suppose, is any musician as good as they want to be, to be like an Eric Clapton or B. B. King? But I enjoyed it and I enjoyed learning. My mother saw my interest and got me guitar lessons, while my brothers learned accordion, but they didn't stay with it. And we had a band for a while through the pub at home. I was the guitar player along with a drummer and singer. We were quite poor, though – I hope there's no recordings!'

Sing-songs and sessions were part and parcel of most pubs' entertainment at one time or another and for the Allens it was no different. 'Twenty-One Years is a Very Long Time' and 'The Old Rustic Bridge by the Mill' and all those old country songs were part of the soundtrack to his life.

From playing in the pub, he moved on to playing in hotels. 'I'm not a great singer but I did some songs, just background music. I was in a band, playing in hotels, playing background music when people would be eating their dinner.'

Playing away in the background seemed to fit his demeanour. You couldn't imagine him as the performer whipping up the crowd.

As he was a talented sportsman, hurling (and football) dominated his days growing up as well. Music faded into the background when Gaelic games arose, which was often. 'I basically grew up in a place with hurling, hurling, hurling as number one. It was my pastime and hobby. I love hurling, I love watching hurling and it was part of my life, but it didn't define me.'

It did, however, show him the wider world as, when he made the Cork teams of the 1970s and 1980s (winning an All-Ireland hurling medal as a substitute in 1978 and winning a league medal with the footballers in 1980, as well as All-Ireland club medals with St Finbarr's in 1980 and 1981), he got to travel to America. It was his first time out of Ireland.

'The fact that I was born in the '50s, we were never out of the country. I wasn't out of the country on holidays until I was probably twenty-one or so. Then I was involved with the Cork teams, got to America and this was a huge culture shock to somebody who had never been out of Ireland, who had never been on a plane before and to suddenly find yourself in LA or San Francisco, or New York, Boston, Chicago. That had an influence as well.'

It was to be a lasting influence, instilling a love of travel, new cultures and experiences.

'I always had an interest in geography. I always remember having maps when I was eight or nine and seeing places – these far-flung places – on the maps. Then, when I got to the age that I could go and I had the money to go, I would be off.'

Vietnam is a particular favourite but then, closer to home, so too is London – again because of the music in the West End. He likes to do his own thing, to travel alone, sourcing the places and accommodation himself, free to come and go as he pleases.

While his playing career saw him play for the Cork seniors in hurling and football, he was still very much his own man, perhaps not driving on as obsessively as others.

'I would have always tried keeping in my life a sense of "this is only sport", even when I was playing myself. I was lucky that I played with teams that were successful for both club and county, but obviously you lost matches along the way as well, and that never phased me or caused me to go into a depression. I've seen fellas go into depression for a day or two or even three; they can't even come out of the house because they are so cut up about a loss. And I can understand that, as some people really put a huge amount into it. But I just felt this was always "just sport" and I still don't think it's too serious, even though I know that people take it very seriously.'

It was something he had to be conscious of when he started writing a column for *The Irish Times*, post-management, because being flippant or taking the mickey out of the sport was not what fans wanted.

'At the time I was thinking this can't be that serious. It was just so serious when I was involved that I couldn't see the wood for the trees. Now that I could write about it I could actually articulate: look, it's not that serious, why are we all so bloody het up about this thing?'

Likewise, if someone had told him when his playing days ended that he would one day be managing the Cork hurlers on All-Ireland final day, he'd have said no way.

'There was a guy working next to me in the school I taught in for many years who was as interested in sport as I was. We discussed sport every day. And very often I would say to him, "Jesus I would never be an inter-county manager. I wouldn't be ruthless enough, I wouldn't have the passion." Years later, when I'd see him he'd say, "God how wrong you were about that!" But really I fell into inter-county management through a totally different route.'

As ever with Allen, his was the route less travelled. His

entry into management came through the influence of Tony Quinn, a psychotherapist who worked with boxer Steve Collins on his mental training and preparation to help him win the World Super-Middleweight title in 1995.

'Seeing Tony Quinn on *The Late Late Show*, hearing about him and what Steve Collins was saying about him, piqued my interest in psychology. Through that I saw that he was doing courses in Dublin, and I said to myself, right, that will be my starting point.

'Now, management still wouldn't have been of interest to me at that stage. It was more of a growing interest in the psychology of people itself. Plus, I was impressed that Steve Collins, such a successful sportsman, would speak so highly of a man who was dealing in psychology. This was never part of hurling when I was involved and it began to interest me in a sporting context.

'I wasn't interested in being a manager. I wasn't even interested in any team, I saw it just as maybe learning something new. Now, where it was going to take me or what I was going to do with it? I wasn't sure about that. I did the course, enjoyed it and learned a bit from it.

'I came back home at the end of it saying, well, I did that, I know a little bit more now. It also introduced me to books from the new-age gurus, the likes of Tony Robbins, and I read a lot in that whole area.'

Whether he knew it or not, and whether it was on a subconscious level, Allen's growing interest in self-improvement and psychology was to lead him back to his sporting past. A friend, Denis Burns, was manager of the Cork minors at the time and asked him if he would be interested in being a masseur with the team.

Without planning it, Allen was back in the dressing room and team environment. The minors even won the All-Irelands in 1997 and 1998, and he realised that being involved in the management team was something he enjoyed.

Then the seniors came calling ('I suppose they saw me as somebody who knew something about the sport, who was with the minors,' he says modestly) and he was a masseur with Jimmy Barry-Murphy's team when they won the All-Ireland in 1999.

As masseur, you are something of a sounding board for the players who might feel more comfortable discussing issues with someone not directly involved with management. Listening came naturally to him and he had a calming influence on the dressing room.

'I grew up in a pub in a country area, where the pub was off the main road, which meant you had to look after your customers. You had to make sure that your customers were coming in to you because if they weren't there was nobody going to stop passing, so I learned a bit from listening to people inside the bar and maybe holding my counsel and saying nothing, just listening, which I probably got from my mother.'

It gave him a valuable skill set and enabled him to bond

with players when the majority of them might never have heard of his playing days or even realised he had played with Cork at all.

'I also enjoyed the fact that I was going down, giving a rub, staying for training and coming away again. I wasn't in the papers; I hadn't the pressure of picking the team or dropping players.'

In the aftermath of the Cork players' strike in 2002, Dónal O'Grady was appointed hurling manager and Allen's influence was called upon once more, but this time as a selector. The laid-back demeanour of Allen couldn't have contrasted more in the context of that group of Cork hurlers, players such as Donal Óg Cusack and Seán Óg Ó hAilpín who were influenced by the Roy Keane mantra of 'Fail to prepare, prepare to fail'.

They were professional in everything but name in terms of their attitude, training, dedication and commitment to winning with Cork. They expected officials, management and the county board to be of the same mindset and, when it wasn't forthcoming, they went on strike for a better say in the running of things. With players of the calibre of Cusack and Ó hAilpín, men who would have excelled at any sport they chose to dedicate their focus to, it was no surprise that consecutive All-Irelands were won and they were only denied a three-in-a-row by a Kilkenny side in 2006 which went on to win four-in-a-row themselves and are regarded as probably the greatest side hurling has ever seen. Such was the rarefied level on which Cork hurling was operating. Into this mix came the laid-back Allen.

He saw his role in very different terms to that of a regular manager when he was appointed as the man in charge for the 2005 season.

'I came into a successful situation with a successful team and with winners. I really didn't need to be as driven to drive it on. It was a totally different set of demands. The demands I had was in keeping the camp happy, ticking over and moving along.'

Remarkably and with great honesty he does accept that, if it had been any other scenario, he wouldn't have been the man to take over. 'I wouldn't have been the right fella because I wouldn't have been driven enough,' he admits.

In Cork at the time, the drive seemed to come primarily from the players. 'It's the strongest characters in the dressing room who set the tone and unity,' Allen says; there's a self-belief that no manager can put into a team.

Brian Cody in Kilkenny is the obvious counter-example to this and is a template of managerial leadership and drive being reflected in the team. Everything stems from what he enables in the dressing room and on the field of play.

'There's no doubt he [Cody] obviously picks players that reflect his determination and drive,' says Allen. 'He sees in them what he wants to have as team players, or the criteria he wants from his players, and he picks players like that.

'When I was with Limerick we played Kilkenny one night and Brian Cody wasn't there. I felt on the line that night that

Kilkenny were lacking something. Well we beat Kilkenny and while we played well, I felt that there was something missing with the Kilkenny players. They just weren't at the same tempo or pitch because Cody wasn't there.'

What Allen did bring as facilitator and enabler-in-chief to the Cork team was an opportunity for more All-Irelands. They retained their All-Ireland as well as regaining Munster in his first year in charge and went for three-in-a-row in 2006, only to be outdone by Kilkenny by three points.

Having become famous for their self-belief and digging themselves out of tight situations, that loss in 2006 signalled the end of Cork's short-lived dominance and Allen stepped aside.

If his time with Cork was, in Allen's words, 'just following my nose and kind of seeing how things go', then his two seasons in charge of Limerick in 2012 and 2013 were more about truly learning what kind of manager he was and pushing himself outside his comfort zone, as he was no longer in a dressing room used to ticking over and to success.

'What I saw with Limerick was that they had a good U-21 team, their club situation was quite good and they were beginning to break through. I saw a group of young fellas who could be moulded. There was sufficient tradition there and there was big interest in hurling in Limerick.'

For Allen, this was more about being a manager in the role of teacher, shaping and influencing youth, a situation of which he had a lifetime's experience.

'My first job, and even into the second year, was trying to make the players realise that they weren't playing for me. They were playing for themselves, number one. They had to decide that just because they were heroes with their club and they came up through hurling and knew nothing else, that maybe it was time for them to sit down and decide: is it worth it?

'Is it worth what you are giving up in terms of time and commitment, whether or not we will actually achieve anything? I was very high on stressing it both years so that fellas could sit down with themselves and say, "Okay, he's not forcing me to play, he's not demanding anything of me, he's saying you think about this and you see if you want to be a part of this."'

It wasn't about driving them on – it had to, like the Cork situation, come from within. 'I was facilitating them to be as good as they could but I wasn't driving them on, telling them this is the be all and end all, I would never do that.'

The difference with Limerick was the fact that he was a known quantity. Those Limerick players had all seen Cork winning All-Irelands. Donal Óg Cusack and Seán Óg Ó hAilpín were legends of the game and John Allen had been up the steps of the Hogan Stand as a winning manager. Getting buy-in now wasn't going to be hard. They believed in him and what he was doing.

The first season in 2012 saw a first-round defeat to Tipperary, followed by a run through the qualifier system as far as the quarter-finals, beating Laois, Antrim and Clare along the way, before losing by three goals to eventual winners Kilkenny.

By the second year, despite failing to get out of 1B in the league, Limerick ended a seventeen-year wait as they captured Munster for the first time since 1996. They beat a much-fancied Tipp in the semi-final and, of course, Cork were Allen's opponents in the final in Thurles. It was bittersweet for the proud Corkman to be facing his own county and lining up against the red jerseys, but his team had a job to do and they duly did it with a nine-point win.

Beating Tipp and Cork to win Munster was an incredible achievement for the players and management. The team were buying into Allen's thinking and methods.

But for Limerick 2013 is a season tinged with memories of what might have been beyond Munster. It was a year when anything, it seemed, could happen. The big guns were there for the taking. Tipp had fallen in Munster and Limerick were champions. Kilkenny were beaten in Leinster and Dublin were the champions for the first time since 1961. Tipperary were then knocked out in the qualifiers by the Cats, who themselves were beaten by Cork in the quarters. That left an unexpected quartet of Dublin, Cork, Clare and Limerick. Liam MacCarthy was anyone's as Limerick prepared to face Clare in Croke Park.

The two managers on the sideline couldn't have been more different. Clare's Davy Fitzgerald, all tense and wired, coiled up like a highly charged electrical circuit, sparking, letting loose at every hit, mistake and questionable decision. Meanwhile, Limerick's John Allen was philosophical, composed, stoic and calm.

A slow start from Limerick in the first half saw them hit ten wides and playing catch-up. They trailed by seven points when the half-time whistle blew. As the players ran off down the tunnel, there was the remarkable sight of Allen and his selectors remaining on the sideline for the next eight minutes as they discussed how to make things right.

Despite handing free-taking duties to sub Shane Dowling, and opening the second half with three unanswered points, Limerick weren't able to kick on and Clare maintained their grip on the game, running out 1–22 to 0–18 winners.

Limerick had lost the 2007 final to Cody's all-conquering Kilkenny, but with this 2013 semi-final it felt like a bigger opportunity had slipped through their fingers. Clare were magnificent in their unlikely run to become All-Ireland champions, but any of the other three teams in the semis knew it could have been them. After all, how often does the All-Ireland hurling championship get to the last four without a Tipperary or Kilkenny looming large? The mid-1990s was the last time the dominance of the 'big counties' was broken and that period had also involved heartbreak for Limerick, with Offaly beating them by six points in the 1994 All-Ireland final, while Wexford won by just two points two years later. Despite the incredible Munster success, 2013 proved to be another year where Limerick fell painfully short. The following year, Kilkenny and Tipperary resumed normal service.

'I don't know why they didn't make the breakthrough,' says Allen. 'You could put your finger on it and say it's one thing or another, but it's not. In Limerick and Waterford's case, they keep striving and keep putting in the time, but they'll only win an All-Ireland once every so often. Why that should happen defies logic, really.

'Yet, there's a core there of players who will just do anything to be on the county team and to try and win something. But, by virtue of the fact that they're not successful a lot of the time, there's a kind of acceptance that we are not any worse than last year, maybe, or we are not worse than any other teams since 1973 in Limerick.'

As he promised the county board, after the two years in charge, John Allen's time was up with Limerick.

'There are managers who love the cut and thrust of it, they love being involved and they will move to different counties, particularly in football where there are more teams. I was never going to be that person, however; the strain and the stress of the whole thing I can do without.'

He dislikes how hurling management can lead you to become one-dimensional. It becomes limiting in its horizons, focus and conversation. It's hurling or nothing, with silences abounding.

Unsurprisingly then, he has no intention of getting back involved and is adamant about that. Besides, he can enjoy his retirement fully now and keeps involved with the game through his *Irish Times* column and TG4 analysis.

But even the years since 2013 have seen a huge leap in the game's evolution and development, he believes. At inter-county level, at least, it is increasingly becoming a foreign arena no longer recognisable from when he was playing and managing.

Strength and conditioning were only really coming into the game when he was with Limerick, but from 2014 on their role has become much more striking and even threatened to take over for a while, much like in Gaelic football, where they have become so important.

The main demand on players is that of their time, as they train like professionals in an amateur sport. The ones who will make it are not the ones with the best skill set, but the players who are prepared to accept the huge demands on their time. Giving everything else up is the only way to succeed and it's expected of everyone on the panels. Commitment is absolute.

Are we training robots for the field then? Unthinking and unwavering, with a narrow tunnel focus of what the team needs to achieve? Would a maverick such as Manchester United legend George Best survive the modern sports ethos?

'There is no doubt about it, we are creating robots,' Allen agrees. 'And a George Best wouldn't make the cut any more either. There's no room for somebody that wouldn't train or eat properly, or go to the gym, no matter how good you are. You will still have the Gooches [Kerry football forward,

Colm Cooper] who are talented and have bought into what's needed, because you will not be accepted unless you buy into the whole team ethos. The days of the Fancy Dan not putting the effort in are gone.'

For Allen, in the modern game, it's the U-21 championship that he retains most affection for, comparable in his mind's eye to the céilí bands and dancers during Willie Clancy Week in Miltown Malbay, Co. Clare, who radiate a joy for living in the present.

'There's less cynicism, there's more off the cuff hurling; you don't see sweepers too often. With the senior game, I would say, look, we have got to accept the way the game is and managers and teams are going to try and get to the level that they'll beat Kilkenny, which is the number one target right now and that dictates everything. It dictates how you are going to win an All-Ireland.'

Is the win-at-all-costs mentality one that will damage the game, however? Hurling, Allen believes, is becoming increasingly like Gaelic football and attending a championship football match for the first time in years brought it home to him just how different a sport it was to when he played. The game was barely recognisable, with players moving all around the field.

The re-emergence of Tipp and Kilkenny, counteracting defensive systems, has been refreshing for lovers of the game and while sweeper systems can be effective, perhaps the reality is, they will only take you so far, providing a solidity to build from, which Waterford looked to do in 2016, coming so close to beating Kilkenny in the semi-final.

'The game has changed. There's no doubt the game has changed,' Allen believes. 'The game is faster, players are fitter, players can strike longer, it's all about possession. Do I like it as a game? I do, of course; I admire the skill that's in the game. I admire the intelligence the players need to have, more so now where they are trying to keep possession of the ball and getting the ball into position for shooting at goal. But the off the cuff hurling that we saw Kilkenny doing up to relatively recently, again if you look at the games of the '60s or '70s or '80s, you saw a different game. You saw skill levels, I suppose, a lot the same, but you had more ground hurling, you had more overhead hurling, now it's about handling the ball and possession.'

Despite the fresh hope with Tipperary's success and swaggering style of 2016 and the hope by many that Kilkenny's dominance has been broken for the good of the game, hurling fans still need to be wary and counties such as Limerick, Clare or the counties below them need to keep on their toes so that the wheels don't fall off.

The role of the manager is also changing. More often now, while being the person who pulls the strings, the manager is not the one actually coaching the team. Plus there are the stats people, the people to do the strength and conditioning (S&C), there's a coach, there's a nutritionist and a psychologist.

The days of the manager ranting and raving are also gone,

it would seem – though Davy Fitzgerald's continued involvement perhaps suggests otherwise. Hurling (and Gaelic football) seems to be nearly going towards a rugby model, whereby the plans are put in place beforehand by management and it is then the players' role to execute these plans on the field of play and adapt to the changes in the game.

The players should be the ones having an influence and input on the game plan, Allen believes. At underage level, coaches and managers should also be developing players to think more for themselves. It is the ability to think for oneself that will make the player stand out. Answers shouldn't always be provided by the manager, Allen argues, and the players should be involved in helping to provide solutions from training to pre-game, half-time and post-match.

During the games, Allen, for one, thinks the manager has no place or influence on the sideline and could just as easily be in the stands observing from on high, just as in rugby. Besides, he says, in big matches with big crowds it's hard for players to hear managers' instructions.

'Up to a few years ago when players went out onto the field and they played within minutes, they were driven on for those few minutes by the manager ranting and raving to win the first contact and to set the tone.

'Nowadays, you might be on the field for forty minutes before the game starts. The warm-up is so comprehensive now that anything you would have said as a manager in the dressing room is well gone by the time the ball is thrown in.

So it's like the famous Muhammad Ali quote that "The fight is won or lost far away from witnesses – behind the lines, in the gym, and out there on the road, long before I dance under those lights."

'It's about not being dependent on some manager using bad language to try and get you annoyed to be better than you actually are. To be preparing properly, to have the goal. Preparing properly to be at the standard that you need to be at. That's more important.'

How then do you get the best out of players? Inspirational quotes or newspaper cuttings are still used in the dressing room, and, for Allen, it's about releasing that 'light in their heads. It might be a book you send his way, or it might be a kind word you had used. We all like to be thought well of and if I know I can put a good word into somebody's ear about something that he is interested in, that makes them feel good. And sure that can only be good for me and them and the team.

'I would have always made a point, particularly on the morning of big games, of being extremely positive and talking about how lucky they were to be there and how lucky I was to be there. How we were the ones inside the white lines, that we had put in all the time and were the lucky people.'

It's about thinking towards success rather than failure and, by nature, John Allen is a positive person who will see the best in people. He has written before about how it isn't the managers' speeches or insights that he remembers from his playing days, but how they made him feel.

It's also about knowing people, knowing what they were doing, knowing what was going on in their lives outside of sport. It's about opening them up to something different, new and unexpected, something he has tried and done successfully down through the years in the classroom.

'I would have always had a philosophy that, every year, I would introduce the school children to something different or new because you never knew if it might trigger off something in a pupil. It could be anything from cooking, to fixing a puncture in a tyre, or maybe taking a hard drive out of a computer.

'The last school I was in, Paschal Sheehy from RTÉ came out and brought a cameraman with him and spent the day in the school taking footage with some of the kids, then editing the package which was aired on RTÉ that evening. It wasn't a big thing, but maybe because of it, there might be one or two kids who will have an interest and go down that route in their lives because of that experience.'

As a teacher, coach or manager, when dealing with kids, he firmly believes that one should be imparting important life values such as humility, sincerity and integrity. It is about the bigger picture and recognising that sport is just one part of that. Life is everything else surrounding it but sport can help us learn and forge the values needed for a fulfilling life. Life is about the journey and the experiences along the way. Find what interests you and see where it takes you. Try out new things and new places, you never know what you may find when you get there.

'There', for John Allen, is a myriad of things and experiences. The hurling management chapter in his life has been closed but there's still so much he wants to see and do. Hurling is just one part of what life has to offer. There is a much wider world to embrace.

Hurling will always be there, in one way or another. He's sure of that. But so will the other great passion in his life: music. That dropped into the background when hurling took over – although he was always strumming away on the guitar for half an hour in the evening when he could grab it. He describes it as a form of mindfulness for himself, a way of switching off, if only for a short while. This was particularly useful when he wanted an escape from the intensity of inter-county hurling management.

'When I was managing teams I did play a good bit, nearly every night before games, I would sit and play. Whatever you have done, wherever you are, I find that whenever I'm playing music, time doesn't matter. I don't notice time which means I am in the moment, my mind is in it.'

He also gets to travel more now that the summers are his again. He likes to disappear for jaunts on his own, which comes, he supposes, from being involved with teams for so long that he just needs that experience of being alone again. Just himself, away from it all.

Before we leave he tells me of a trip coming up that combines his love of music and travel. He is going on a road trip across the USA to New Orleans, Nashville and the Deep South.

For all the talk of All-Irelands, Munster championships and inter-county hurling, this is when John Allen truly lights up. The softness in his voice raises a little, and the passion and excitement comes through as he takes me through the itinerary he has planned: from the jazz of New Orleans, on to the Cajun heartlands, then on up to Mississippi and the blues, before hitting rock and roll in Memphis, country music in Nashville and maybe even a detour to Alabama for a bit of history.

It's a 700km journey from New Orleans to Nashville that will take him three weeks or more. He will drive alone and stay with jazz musicians and in Airbnbs, but he will have an iPod full of music accompanying him every step of the way. Much like in the Mississippi river that he will be following upstream from Louisiana, there will be bends along the way, but he expects it and he's okay with that.

There's some kind of plan in the background but you also have to see where the bends in the river will take you. They took him from a rural pub in Cork to GAA fields to Croke Park and beyond. For thirty-six years it anchored him in a school in Togher in Cork city and at other times he set sail, developing an interest in psychology, which led him back to hurling dressing rooms and the experience of management.

'I was in the right place at the right time. I wouldn't dream of dressing it up any other way,' he says modestly. 'I do appreciate that I am extremely fortunate and that as long as my health is okay and my family are okay, well then, life is good and it is really good too. I am in a very good place.'

He's still in the right place because the right place and time for Allen is now, while being positive and open to whatever is in front of you. Hurling was one part but there's so much more.

The open road from New Orleans awaits and there's no real ending in sight. For John Allen, from music to sport and teaching, that is the real beauty in life.

9

Hunger:
ANTHONY DALY

The you you see, will be the you you'll be.

'No longer the whipping boys!' went up the yell from the stand in Páirc Uí Chaoimh on that July summer's day in 1997.

Clare captain Anthony Daly had just led his team to a remarkable Munster final victory over Tipperary by three points. It was their second Munster championship in three years. Their win in 1995 had erased years of hurt stretching back to 1932. But they hadn't beaten Tipp, so long their tormentors, along the way. Two years later, Anthony Daly felt as if the tag of 'nearly men' had finally been shed.

Clare, so long seen as the scrappy underdogs to the aristocrats of Tipperary and Cork, had broken through and proven to their rivals, the province, the country and to themselves that they deserved their place alongside them.

For Anthony Daly, growing up obsessed with hurling

as a young fella in Clarecastle, it was always about proving yourself, scrapping as the underdog to overcome the odds. Having the self-belief was one thing, making it happen when it was needed most was what was always lacking.

But trace his journey back further and you can see the beginnings of what he would bring onto the pitch as a leader and afterwards as a manager.

'I was obsessed with dressing rooms growing up as a young lad. I was fairly serious about it and while I could have the craic, I didn't have a pint until I was a bit older. I just wanted to make it and concentrate on the hurling. There was a fierce tradition with my uncles and family but when my brothers hit nineteen/twenty they said fuck it and moved on. It was harder then, Clarecastle weren't anything – we went from 1970 to 1986 without winning a championship.'

As is so often the case in these stories, it comes down to timing, when the confluence of a driven few, coupled with ambition, hard work and talent, come together to drive success over the line.

'I was lucky as I came along at a good time. Clarecastle hurling came back to prominence in 1983, winning the county league and then losing the county final in 1984. We won an U-15A in '83 and there were inklings that things were going to happen.'

At the same time, his schooling in St Flannan's College, the hurling hotbed in Ennis that took on all comers in Munster and beyond, was instilling a mindset of success.

'It's about belief, belief, belief. Take St Flannan's. They were winning All-Ireland colleges when I was in primary school and when I went in there as a first year they won the Harty Cup and I felt if I could get on the team I could win a Harty Cup medal too. As sure as night follows day we did.

'The same day we won it, St Pat's from Shannon won the B All-Ireland. We had five Limerick minors and a Tipp minor but the rest of us were all from Clare, as were all the St Pat's lads. We had beaten three Cork schools along the way but then we played Cork two weeks later in the Munster minor semi-final for the county.

'I was playing in the same position as the Harty Cup, marking the very same guy at right corner-back, in the very same venue and yet was the same belief there? I just didn't think we'd beat Cork and sure enough they beat us by two points and Tipp beat them by a point in the Munster final, so there was nothing between us or them. Yet it was Tipp who won Munster and went to the All-Ireland final. It's amazing what the mindset and belief can and will do.'

Daly made his debut for Clare in 1989/90, a tough time for Clare hurling when there were no great expectations. The contrast in going from All-Ireland success at St Flannan's to pulling on the Banner jersey couldn't have been greater. Clare hurling was about just getting by.

'It was stagnant up till Len Gaynor,' Daly admits. 'But Len did an awful lot of work to bring it up to a certain level [from 1990 to 1994]. Then Loughnane had that U-21 team, and the minor team of '89 had got to an All-Ireland final, which was a big thing at the time. There was the likes of the Jamesie O'Connors and the Lohans at U-21 who were starting to show glimpses of what they could achieve.

'But Loughnane drove us, he really drove us. He'd ate you in training and I certainly wouldn't have been as manic or as insulting to players in training when I was a manager later on! The week before the match he'd be telling you he'd never seen you in better shape. He was an absolute psychologist, a genius. Knowing when to use the carrot and when to use the stick, that's man management and you can see in some cases it falls down when not used properly.'

The apex of the Loughnane management came in the famous half-time period of the 1997 All-Ireland final, when Clare were down by four points to Tipperary and Loughnane stepped back to let the players come forward and take owner-ship of the situation.

'We were five or six minutes into our half-time break and there was still no word out of yer man [Loughnane] at all and we were looking around at each other. So myself, [Brian] Lohan and Mike Mac[Namara] started talking. Since he wasn't going to do it we'd better do it, we thought. Brian Lohan really sticks out for me that day, he stood up and started saying "Come on!"

'We were all standing in a circle, roaring at each other, with Loughnane saying nothing, just standing apart from it all near the door. Then there was a knock telling us, "Come on lads, Tipp are on the field." Loughnane stopped us at the door, everyone stopped and stared and spread out a bit around him and with the mad eyes he just said, "Men needed now." I'll never forget it, I'll take it to my grave. "Men needed now."

'We all looked at each other and as I was going out I stopped the lads again in the tunnel and I said, "By Jesus, this is the biggest half of our lives. You heard what he said, he's right lads, we've been wimps for thirty-five minutes." And the next thirty-five minutes were the best of our lives. To be four down, to concede two goals, us not get a goal and still win against that Tipp team was just some thirty-five minutes of hurling.'

It won't always work. Loughnane could have tried it again the following year and lads could say, 'Ah sure, he said that last year.' When it does work, however, it can have a powerful impact.

'I remember a great U-21 final once up in Miltown Malbay with Clarecastle,' recalls Daly. 'I was manager and I had a selector with me, Barney Lynch. We were in the dressing room getting ready and he stopped the boys and wouldn't let them put on their jerseys. "Leave off yer jerseys," he says to them. I was looking at him wondering what the fuck is this all about? We were getting ready to go out and play. "Now," he says. "Everyone put on the jerseys together. Smell the men that went before you. They might be brand new jerseys but they pulled the same black and white over their heads. Sixty, seventy, eighty years ago, the same men – yer grandfathers, and great-grandfathers did it." Jesus the hairs on the back of my neck stood up there and then ... but now, try it again with another team and it could be a waste of time. It's about the moment, reading it and capturing it in the right way.'

Can such management be learned or quantified? What is it about some managers, who can lead and have a dressing room of players go through walls for them?

But what has been built up over time can also be lost just as quickly. How to stay relevant and have one's message count every season is the key to longevity. Alex Ferguson at Manchester United moved the players on regularly to inject fresh blood into the team and keep things from stagnating. Noticeably, he also changed his approach to players, recognising that players in the twenty-first century could no longer be bawled at and given the hair-dryer treatment.

Players may not be quite equals, but they have become more than mere soldiers in the trenches. Perhaps that is why, when Ger Loughnane took over at Galway in 2006 or when Babs Keating returned to Tipperary the year before, those stints were unsuccessful. What worked for one generation will not necessarily work for the next.

Brian Cody's legacy at Kilkenny has cemented his ability to rubber-stamp a philosophy, a structure and a mindset that run through the hurling veins of the county. But it's not some secret sauce or magic wand he's waving to make it happen.

'Brian Cody doesn't seem to do anything different,' says Daly. 'When I was playing and managing there was a code of *omertà* there, you'd find out nothing. In later years I've got to know Eddie Brennan and Henry Shefflin with *The Sunday Game* and you'd meet them at various things and you'd be quizzing them up and down. But nothing seems to change; it's the same formula; it works and it doesn't change. Cody has created this aura about them even though it wasn't always there.'

Because of the incredible success under Cody for nearly twenty years, it's easy to forget that, on the field anyway, they weren't always as feared.

'One of my first league games when I started playing was against Kilkenny in Ennis,' says Daly. 'John Moroney, who had played in the '86 Munster final and was the catalyst for us beating Tipp in '95, was a great guy loved by everybody, but was killed in a car crash in late '93. He was a quietly spoken guy but fellas looked up to him. [Len Gaynor recalled years afterwards in *The Irish Times* how Moroney's death affected the team. "Lads were hurt and when they looked at their hurling afterwards they had a sense of urgency. Life is pretty short after all."] I was playing corner-back and John was full-back. He was telling me, "Dalo, the thing about this crowd is, you don't have to be worrying about fellas timbering. These crowd play ball, they're soft; you can be dishing it out a bit here." Then contrast that to twenty years later where their corner-forwards are probably tougher than their corner-backs. Cody has created this culture and it has continued on. If the person who is driving that success and mindset from the top moves on, it can be lost very quickly and it can be toxic from the top right down to underage and very hard to get back.

'Take St Flannan's, who are now in a trough and just can't get it going. Young lads are saying "I've Harty training but I'll go training with the club." Missing Harty training! In my time, if you didn't go, there'd be forty fellas there before you. Now it seems they're struggling to get an interest in it. The problem is if you let it drop. That's the key with Kilkenny, they never let it drop.'

If the skill set isn't that different between the top counties and players, the only difference is the culture and mindset. As well as being the current Limerick minor team manager, Daly is also involved with UL as Freshers' manager. Therefore, he is in a prime position to see how players from different counties react on the bigger stages.

'We had a very good lad from Laois who came for the trials in UL. We were trying to pick two squads out of the 126 lads invited down for the trials and this lad stood out right away. We brought him onto the Fresher 1s but then we played Sixmilebridge seniors in a challenge match and LIT in the league and he didn't sparkle at all, he didn't go to the ball.

'The boys were saying it's all happening a bit quicker now for him and that's why he's struggling, but I said, "No lads, it's all up here in the mind; I'm convinced it's all mental for him." He's surrounded by minors from around Munster, Wexford, Galway and he might be thinking, "What am I doing here?" So, we dropped him down to the Fresher 2s, to midfield, where he was outstanding against UCC, scoring about 1–3 from midfield and he's a contender to go back up for the championship. I saw nothing in his ability that was less than the other guys' ability, but coming from Laois was he thinking differently to the others?'

The expectations of underage Dublin hurlers are another prime example of having no inhibiting mindsets. For the younger guns that got their Leinster breakthrough under Daly in 2013 with Dublin's first senior Leinster hurling title in fifty-two years, it was just another day at the office. They had been used to winning for so long at underage levels that they felt it should be no different at senior level.

'I remember in 2009 when Dublin beat Wexford and it was the first time in nearly twenty years that the county had beaten a recognised "bigger" team. They had overcome the "fear" of Wexford and fellas like Kevin Flynn and Liam Ryan [senior figures on the Dublin panel] were crying and hugging each other with the emotion and feeling of being back in a Leinster final for the first time in eighteen years.

'Yet Liam Rushe [a Dublin underage star] was looking at them thinking, "What the fuck? It's only Wexford." To him, the Dublin teams he'd played on had been beating the Kilkennys from underage up. Wexford haven't beaten them since then either.'

Hurling runs through Daly's veins. It was inevitable he would stay with the game after he retired. Even while he was still playing he got involved in management and training – it always seemed a natural extension for someone as obsessed with the game as he was.

'I was always stuck in the training and coaching side of things, even as a player. I was training U-12 footballers when I was sixteen and when we won the All-Ireland in 1995, myself and the Sparrow [Ger O'Loughlin] trained Clarecastle to the Minor A championship and I was training them when I was an All Star in 1994.

'We were single, living at home, having the craic, giving it all to the county and wouldn't have been playing much with the seniors at the club so we made time. There was six of us from Clarecastle on the panel and I'd be saying to the lads at Clare training, "Hook a sliotar there each of you tonight." Fergie Tuohy would take three, Stephen Sheedy would probably take five, Kenny Morrissey would take one and myself and Sparrow would take one or two and Alan Neville would take one. All of a sudden we'd have this bag full of spanking new All Star sliotars.

'We'd be training the minors at 5.30 p.m. for an hour before heading off to Cusack Park. The seniors would be coming on at 7 p.m. in Clarecastle and Oliver Plunkett, the senior manager, would be saying, "Where are ye getting those fucking sliotars from?" I'd tell him, "Look, we're not charging the club anything for them so mind your own business!"'

Whether it is underage, minor or senior, for Daly it should be about having the right belief, mindset and ambition. It's also about doing it the right way, saying to others, 'This is the way it's done here.'

'With Clarecastle, we have a culture and mindset that's all about playing A, even if we're weak. Now, some people think, what's the point in getting hammered by thirteen goals at U-14 when we could be more competitive in the B and lads wouldn't be getting disillusioned. My thinking, though, is the opposite. We're A. If you're playing for Clarecastle, you're playing A. And if you're getting hammered by thirteen goals? Well, then we've got to work on this, boys, and we're going to work and we're going to help you and you'll be better by U-15.

'In Limerick, with the Forristal Cup [for inter-county U-14s in Munster] team, they got hockeyed at the start but we worked at it and when we faced the holders, Cork, we gave them a battle. It ended up 2–9 to 0–9, with us missing a penalty and Cork scoring one. Cork were in shock, they weren't expecting this, Limerick nearly after beating them. We went on and won the shield [played between the losing counties in the Forristal Cup], beating Tipp and beating Clare in the final.

'Going home with the shield, I said to them, "Do you see now boys where we can go with this?" They're getting there, not quite there yet. But beating Tipp was a huge thing.'

Playing A for Clarecastle or any other club doesn't equate to senior-level success, however, much less making it at inter-county level. There are so many distractions for impressionable young men. Plus, you have to prove you're good enough to displace a hardened and experienced senior who has been in possession of the jersey.

But a conveyor belt of talent has to keep coming through, for the sake of the county team, for the sake of the county, for interest from the fans and for the next generation of kids wanting heroes to look up to and believe in.

Ger Loughnane is critical of the county structures and set-up, believing they don't maximise Clare's ability to scout the future talent. They're looking in the wrong places and at the wrong things, he says. Daly too wonders if the talent will shine through and if they can find a little gem out there somewhere.

'I was watching a Harty Cup game and there was a fella from Doon who was outstanding at centre back against Kilmallock. "Where did this fella come from?" I was asking. Was he not in the academy? They think they have everyone, but even though he went into the academy at U-15 he never went back for U-16s and he was in danger of slipping through. So we've him coming in for a trial for the Limerick minors. You have to be able to do that.

'The reality is, if you get four minors that make it, you're getting a great return. We got virtually nothing from the 1997 team when we won the double that day [senior and minor All-Irelands were captured by Clare on a historic day] because our lads were still there. Then in 1999, although the minors didn't win anything, out of that group we got Tony Griffin, Tony Carmody, Gerry Quinn, Conor Plunkett, Diarmuid McMahon and Andrew Quinn. Because they didn't win they probably wanted it more, they forced their way in. Gerry Quinn even took my place for a finish in 2001, getting number seven.'

By that stage Daly's playing time was coming to an end and the writing was on the wall. Loughnane had moved on, as had some of the older guard. When Loughnane's replacement, Cyril Lyons, picked the team and told him, 'Dalo you're not starting', Daly was honest enough to accept that he probably didn't put enough effort in earlier in the year. But he still believed in himself and that his time wasn't yet up, and for three months he bust a gut to get himself ready for the championship. He still didn't start, however, and Tipp beat them by a point.

'I was a bit thick that day because I felt I could have been brought on and used. But that night myself and Cyril had a few pints and the following day as well and I told Cyril, "Listen, I was wrong there and completely out of order." In fairness, Cyril said, "Dalo, I should have brought you on, you would have lifted the whole crowd and if I had my time over …" But as a manager you make decisions on the spur of the moment.'

After twelve years, three Munster titles and two All-Irelands, his playing time was up. Clare reached another All-Ireland final the following year without him, this time losing to Brian Cody's Kilkenny, and it was to be Cyril Lyons' last season in charge.

Only having been gone from the game a short while, Daly was appointed Clare manager in 2003. He had been managing Clarecastle, taking them to a county final and with his leadership skills and popularity within the county it seemed a natural next step for him to take.

Was it too soon and too much to ask for one who had so recently retired and still had much to learn in the art of management? Probably, in hindsight, but the chance was there and he was going to grab it with both hands.

It was a case of what-ifs and close calls for the manager, although a nineteen-point mauling at the hands of Waterford in his first game in the Munster championship put him on the back foot from the start. Clare, however, did take Kilkenny to a replay in the All-Ireland quarter-finals before losing by five points.

The following year they exited Munster at the first hurdle before reaching the All-Ireland semis, losing by a point to a Cork team who completed their two-in-a-row that year. It was to be more of the same in his final year in charge, with failure in Munster before another semi-final defeat to the eventual winners, this time Kilkenny.

'The time with Clare was so demanding, going for All-Irelands especially. And the Cork game, the All-Ireland semi-final in 2005, was so close it was torture. Six points up with fourteen minutes to go and losing it by one – absolute torture. Then we really rattled Kilkenny in 2006, two points in it with seven minutes to go. We were really in that game going down the stretch and had them rattled, we put everything – life and soul – into that game. I'd persuaded Lohan and Seanie to give it another year and they did and they trained like two lunatics and Seanie was captain … and just … the utter devastation … and … I don't know …'

It's the one time the emotion, despair and regrets are still visible in his eyes and audible in his breathing, as he thinks about the what-ifs.

Predictably, the criticism and flak came at him when neither Munster nor All-Ireland success was forthcoming. What hurt most, perhaps, was the fact that the most stinging and vocal criticism came from his old mentor, Loughnane.

'Ger was OTT in his criticism of my regime,' says Daly. 'There was a bit of a stand-off for a year or so when he took sides in things that I felt he shouldn't have got involved in. The gas thing was, I was doing everything modelling it on his management style. I'd had four or five county managers when he took over and I saw this was the successful way so I was going to try and model myself on it.'

This comes back to the importance of not being anyone else's man but your own. How much of the art of hurling management can actually be learned and how much is intrinsic psychology and people skills?

He needed to get back to basics after Clare, to step away from the limelight and the back-biting. He needed to remind himself of what hurling was all about when he was just a Clarecastle player. He found it across the Shannon harbour in Kilmoyley, north Kerry. In Kilmoyley village there's one pub, the pitch, the church and a graveyard with houses and farms scattered about the district.

North Kerry has always been the traditional hotbed of hurling in the Kingdom. Close enough to be influenced by

Limerick and Clare, it has always stood apart from the more cosmopolitan, southern part of the county where football reigns. In Kilmoyley, every kid that goes through the national school is playing hurling and part of the local club. They maximise the talent but, most importantly, they foster a deep commitment to who and what their village stands for.

'Their love of hurling down there is incredible,' Daly explains. 'It's more than just hurling, it's a huge part of the whole identity and more than just the love of the game. You really smell the tribalism and there's a huge cultural difference between them and south Kerry. If I had the price of a holiday home I wouldn't be buying it in Kenmare or Killarney; I'd be buying it in Ballyheigue. I prefer the people there; they're less calculated, less of the Pat Spillane-ism about them!'

When he told people that he was going to be managing Kilmoyley, the reaction was one of, 'Kerry hurling? What are you doing that for?'

'They thought I was crazy but I won back-to-back titles in Kerry and what a time it was.'

Leaving his home at 5.50 p.m. he'd be on the 6 p.m. ferry at Kilrush and be across the harbour and in Kerry by half-past. On the pitch at 7, training at 7.15. Afterwards, he'd be out the gate at 8.30, have two pints of Heineken at Tarbert waiting for the boat to come in, get the last ferry home and be back into work in his pub, Murty Browne's in Tullycrine, at 10 p.m. It all ran like clockwork.

'Kilmoyley was so good for me before I went to Dublin. It refreshed me and got me back to basics. I remember the first night I stayed below, it was after about three months. We had won the county league semi-final and it was a Saturday night. Maurice McElligott, a selector with me, said, "Sure, can't you stay over Saturday night and we might bring them out for a couple of pints? There'll be no final played till the end of the year."

'"Jaysus, I might stay for a few beers so," I said.

'We all went out for a few beers and it was then I was asking them about the national school, the parish, that sort of thing. From then on there was a bond and I went down to see them when they were in the county final again in 2015 even though I wasn't managing them any more. I wouldn't mind, but our [Clarecastle] minors were in the minor A final that day too. But I'd given my word and I was trying to listen to Clare FM in the car radio down in Tralee, barely able to get a signal. I had to go on the phone to hear it and we were two points up and I let a roar off in the car in the car park. People were looking at me, wondering who's this lunatic roaring out of the car? I went in, anyway, full of the joys at the minors winning, but also half guilty I'd missed that.

'I was asked to go into the Kilmoyley dressing room and say a few words. "Would you come in?" they asked me.

'"I will yeah, I'll come in, I'll be there," I said and Jesus the emotion that was there. It meant so much to them, I used to be trying to calm them down beforehand. I went into the dressing room and tears were running down their faces – and this was before the game.'

The three years in Kerry were a breath of fresh of air, away from the cauldron of senior inter-county hurling, but it was time to step back into the fire. He chose to do so with the county arguably most in the media glare: Dublin. If Kilmoyley had been a reminder of the tradition and community spirit around the game, Daly was now going back into the modern world of science, stats and analysis.

This is the side of the modern game that traditionalists see as a foreign field, where science dominates preparation and game plans. For Daly, however, you can't compare hurling management in the twenty-first century to the 1980s or 1990s.

'It's much harder nowadays to get success,' Daly believes. 'When I first started playing for Clare, there was zero science, training was only half-throttle and there was a drinking culture. But now every county out there, from the Christy Ring teams up, has the science and are all training savage. Ninety per cent of it is go for the ball, work on your touch, be brave and have confidence in yourself, which can also be a hard thing to quantify.

'I would have gone in depth into it with different guys we dealt with in the Dubs and with Clare. "The you you see, will be the you you'll be", that sort of thing. You decide what you want to be. "You're already the Leinster champions" the Dublin hurlers were being told early in 2013. "You're the Leinster champions. You are!" And we hadn't even pucked a ball yet.

'The younger generations are buying into this level of mental preparation and science around the game now. The levels of professionalism I see in UL are phenomenal, from the high performance gym to everything that's being developed there; it is all available to them. I have four Galway minors, five Limerick minors, four Clare minors, three Kilkenny lads, a Wexford and Waterford minor and they're all going back to their own counties with the information and knowledge of what the others are doing.

'They're going back and saying, "Do you know what the Galway U-21s were doing last week? They were in Coole Park and they swam across the lake, out the other side into ice baths and jacuzzis. And what are we at? Nothing!" That's the kind of information that's being shared across the counties and squads.

'My generation didn't go to college much, you see, and didn't have the same interaction with other players. I did three months studying electronics in LIT and hated it, before I was offered a job in the bank in Ennis. It was a no-brainer for me, but lads are staying on in college doing degrees and masters. The Dubs' Liam Rushe went working for the first time last year aged twenty-five or twenty-six – "Welcome to the real world, Rushie!" I said to him.'

The danger is, and it's an accusation thrown at the modern game – and all sports as well – that kids and players are being over-coached and over-drilled, and spontaneity and instinct are being coached out of them.

With so much information easily accessible and being

shared across countries and sports, there is the concern of 'conformist coaching' developing, with coaches all learning from the same playbook and imparting the same rote messages to kids up and down the country.

For Daly, though, there is a lot to be learned from the sharing of information and insights.

'To say it's not useful is wrong. I've a notebook at home where I'd be taking down notes of stuff I've seen from the likes of Tommy Dunne [former Tipp and Dublin coach] and there's any amount of lads I've met who've asked me about stuff and I'd be telling them "This is how it's done." However, you have to say that at certain times with a team it can be about not getting beaten. "Don't get beaten" is a manager-driven thing, I accept that.'

But there is a kickback against the defensive, sweeper style of play, he says, and he believes the game is going to become even more expansive.

'I still think the way hurling is, the way you can launch a sliotar over the bar from a hundred yards, the game won't become like Gaelic football.'

There is a lot more changing and tweaking of the game and players and positions now than when he was playing.

'I often said, wasn't it grand to be there on a Tuesday or a Wednesday when the teams were announced and I was working in the bank and I knew who I was marking come the weekend. Now you haven't a fuckin' clue who you're marking!

'Nowadays, you have to be ready for anything. It's like

total hurling, corner-backs have to be able to go up and score, be every bit as skilful and be just as able to punish teams with scores. But I do think the game is getting better and better for it. I've never seen a better game in my life than the 2014 drawn final between Kilkenny and Tipp and that goes back to the 1970s, '80s, '90s.'

The demise of the provincial competitions, however, has sucked some of the life, the excitement and rivalries out of the game. With the back-door system, getting knocked out of the Munster championship doesn't have the same pain and finality; teams are now looking to peak, not for their provinces, but for the All-Ireland quarters and beyond. In Leinster, meanwhile, the decline of Wexford and Offaly has degraded the Leinster championship, although, for a short time at least, Dublin did begin to threaten Kilkenny.

'I certainly felt in my time there was a bit of a rivalry between Dublin and Kilkenny building up,' Daly agrees. 'We beat them in a replay [the 2013 Leinster semi-final], the only replay Cody ever lost, and beat them in a league final.'

As to the quality coming through, Daly believes that the Kilkenny hegemony can be toppled, with the likes of Dublin and Limerick winning an All-Ireland in the next ten years.

'Plus Fitzy will give Wexford a major lift. I see them coming out of 1B quickly enough and anything could happen after that. They could land in a Leinster final and easily be in an All-Ireland semi-final. It doesn't take that much to get the whole thing lifted.

'Now everyone wants to be winning the All-Ireland and while it's good, all I dreamt about growing up was seeing Clare win a Munster championship and then people ask me, "Was your time with Dublin really a success when you only won Leinster?" And yet every night in Parnell Park when we walked out, I'd tip the picture of the men of '61 [when Dublin last won the Leinster hurling title] and I'd say to the boys before we'd be leaving to go into the big ones, especially in 2013, "Tip the '61 boys, lads, we're going to be the next ones."'

Dublin have been threatening to be a force in hurling for years. Their population size, their commercial clout, the passionate hurling people, as well as the long-term plans and structures put in place since the early 2000s mean many pundits have been touting a Dublin hurling All-Ireland someday soon.

Daly's arrival as Dublin manager for the 2009 season was to be the catalyst for ending the barren years and bringing through the underage talent and success to senior county level. In much the same way that Loughnane ended the perennial underachievement in Clare, Anthony Daly was expected to end it for the capital.

After six years in charge is it fair to argue that, until Liam MacCarthy is won and consistency in success is delivered, Dublin hurling will always be seen as underachieving? It's an accusation that makes Daly bristle.

'If you'd told me before I took over that I'd win a National League and a Leinster title, I'd have said "Fucking hell!"

Especially after my first match in charge, a Walsh Cup game early in the year against Kilkenny in Parnell Park, when Brian Cody arrived up with half a team and it finished 6–18 to 0–17 for Kilkenny.

'Driving home to Clare that night I was thinking to myself: what have I let myself in for here? This is going to be a hard gig. If you'd told me that same evening that in the next five years we'd be in three Leinster finals, win one, win a league, two Walsh Cups, be in an All-Ireland quarter-final, stay up in Division One except for one year, I'd have taken the hand off you and said that's savage. But yet ...'

But yet, they didn't kick on?

'There was a massive opportunity in 2011. Winning the league came a bit out of the blue and we were a bit fortunate. We beat Cork down in Cork that day and Waterford beat Galway in Waterford. We only barely beat Cork and the next thing is we ended up in the league final against Kilkenny because of the league table system. With due respect, Kilkenny were not at full throttle but Dublin being there was a bit of novelty to them, "Ah sure it's Dublin, we'll be beating them along the way."

'They'd beaten us in the Leinster final in 2009 when I played a sweeper. It wasn't a bad performance, 2–18 to 0–18, six points in it, but we weren't ready for them yet. However, in winning the league in 2011, we beat Waterford, Tipp, Offaly and Galway. When we beat Offaly in Tullamore I remember leaving Tullamore that night and we had to have a garda escort to get out of the place. All along the road there were lines and lines of Dublin cars with kids beside them pucking balls and Dublin jerseys everywhere. I turned to Richie Stakelum [Dublin selector] and said, "Jesus, there's something happening here kid."

'Then the Leinster final against Kilkenny a few months later was a bit of, "Here's the backlash" and sure enough they beat us by eleven points. But, the psychology again – we let it feed into our heads that the big bad wolf was going to come back. It was hugely psychological and some lads admitted afterwards that they were beaten before they went out. However, we still recovered and beat Limerick and for Dublin to beat Offaly, Galway, Limerick and win the league, and run Tipp, who had put seven goals past Waterford, to four points in an All-Ireland semi-final, that was a great year for us.

'In 2012 everyone expected things to happen but somehow that game against Kilkenny in Portlaoise just killed us [Dublin lost 2–21 to 0–9]. It's akin to heavyweight title fights or [Conor] McGregor's fights. There's all the build-up and the press conferences and all that, but then you've to strip to your waist, go toe to toe and fight the fight. We just didn't fight the fight, but we were way better than that.'

The Dublin players might have been hurlers when he took over, but they weren't battle-hardened or battle-scarred, with too much of what Daly calls the 'wipe-me-arse mentality' prevalent. Toughening them up had been one of his first goals and weekends in the Glen of Imaal doing army endurance camps was one way he achieved this. To be fair to the players, they took it on the chin and they buckled down with whatever was thrown at them.

That was the character part. But what of the skills? Daly saw a preponderance of 'textbook coaching', which had left a legacy of players not being coached properly in some basic skill sets. For example, many of the players had a preference for the roll lift.

'If I could put my hands on the fella who coached them that …' he says through gritted teeth. 'That was their first bad habit. Jab lifting is much more effective because you're moving forwards and on the run. Roll lifting you have to be static and you're nearly backing out. The only time I ever roll lifted in my life was taking a free. We were street coached, you see.

'The Na Fianna lads [the Drumcondra-based Dublin GAA club] were the worst for it. They were great lads to have and they'd die for you, but we used to have war over it. It's so hard to un-train those kinds of habits. It's about good hurling habits. "You can spend all the time you like with coach-to-player time but it's what you do on your own that will make you a player," says Frank Rijkaard.

'When I started playing hurling you'd nearly have been laughed at, but St Flannan's made it sexy by winning All-Ireland colleges medals. You think back to Shane O'Donnell in 2013 [Clare's All-Ireland hero], the long hair, from the town, good-looking, the three goals, he had it all. My own girls who were teenagers couldn't believe it when they got his autograph and picture. That's the sort of thing that can bring the game on but it can disappear just as quick.'

There were plenty of ups and downs over the six years Daly was in charge of Dublin and the promise and potential of hurling in Dublin is still there, Daly believes; it's just being overshadowed by the footballers who, under Jim Gavin, are regarded as one of the greatest sides ever.

It's been a brave move by Dublin, Daly believes, making players decide after the age of sixteen whether they want to concentrate on football or hurling, and it's something that he agrees with.

'It had to happen in Dublin because they were coming out of minor and the glamour of football was being dangled in front of them with talk of scholarships and this kind of thing. I heard it all back and the key guys picked the football of course – Ciarán Kilkenny was always telling me that hurling was his favourite game and he just wanted to hurl.

'But we had a couple of victories also. The two Schutte guys were approached about football and they laughed at them. "No," they told them, "hurling is my game." It's a case of "I don't care if I never win anything with the hurlers; I'm a hurler, that's my game."'

With the footballers overshadowing the hurlers at senior level, it's easy to forget that in 2016 Dublin were Leinster U-21 and minor champions in hurling, but didn't win either of the two in football. The danger in Dublin, however, is that the pool of talent is too concentrated on just a few clubs.

'After Dotsy [O'Callaghan], there's nobody coming from Finglas and there's nobody out of Tallaght, while there's nobody north of O'Tooles [the Ayrfield-based club],' Daly cautions. 'It was five clubs who were giving us everything. That needs to widen out.'

All the same, a first league title since 1939 and a first Leinster since 1961 were won under Daly's time in charge. A lot of players and managers came and went in between those fifty-plus years, but it took years of underage development before it came to fruition at senior level. The holy grail of the All-Ireland has to be next for the county's ambitions.

Meanwhile, Daly has gone back to youth. It is a joy for him to work with Limerick's minors, impressionable players with their futures ahead of them. Plus, they gave him his first taste of an All-Ireland final since 1997 when reaching the minor final in 2016 against Tipp.

'Going in under the Cusack Stand was a huge thing that brought it all back to me and I thanked the lads for giving me the chance to be back involved again.'

It was a chastening experience, however, a far cry from the 1997 days, with Tipp winning by seven points this time around.

'While they were crying and in bits in the dressing room afterwards, I was able to say to them, "Be gutted, let it all feed in, you need to feel gutted, but have a bit of pride as well. You didn't let your families or your clubs down. You did in the Munster final seven weeks ago when you let yourselves, your families, your clubs and the jersey down, but you didn't today and everyone is proud of you."

'If everyone can look each other in the eye afterwards and say they gave it everything, that's what matters. It won't go everyone's way but they didn't seize up like they did in the Munster final. Everyone went for the ball in the All-Ireland and though we missed our two goal chances, we created them and went for it. That's what you want.'

He's back in college as well, studying sports psychology. It says something about Daly that his hunger for the game is as strong as ever.

'You have to stay involved to keep relevant,' he says. 'You have to be watching, seeing what tactics are being used, and you have to be really studying it.'

It's more than the study, however; it's even more than the belief and mindset. It goes much deeper than that.

'There's just something about it, I can't explain it. I can't wait for Sunday to see even our U-15s in the county final. I'm mad to go up and watch them. I'm as buzzed about that.'

10

Identity:
TERENCE 'SAMBO' McNAUGHTON

Sometimes we try to put the roof on the house before there's a foundation in place. You must get the foundations right first.

For hurling people, it's about more than a game; it's a passion and culture they can't imagine their lives without. It intersects their daily living, it occupies their minds and, in many cases, it's what has driven them to excel.

But when we talk about passion and identity we do so in a sporting context only. For Terence 'Sambo' McNaughton from Cushendall, Co. Antrim, however, and so many GAA men and women growing up playing Gaelic games in Northern Ireland during the Troubles, it stood for something more. It was a badge of identity, of pride in your community and culture; it showcased your place in a contested state.

It was also a badge to mark you out as being from the

nationalist community. Some unionist politicians even went so far as to call the GAA the 'sporting wing of the IRA'.

When you had the British Army base taking over part of Crossmaglen's ground in south Armagh, when GAA players were being harassed, assaulted and even killed because of their sport, it's hard for anyone who didn't live through those times and experience it first-hand to know what the GAA, and hurling especially, meant to people like Sambo McNaughton.

Sambo is a hurling man first and foremost, like everyone else featured in this book, but for him, growing up with hurling meant so much more – it was about constantly looking over your shoulder to see what might be coming at you.

'Our brothers in the GAA didn't really understand,' he says. 'Walking down the street with a hurley was like a target on your back. The game was secondary, really, during the Troubles. Knowing you couldn't wear a jersey in certain parts of town or even, when I was hurling at minor level, our hurleys would have to be dropped off at certain points.

'The first day I met my wife, the British Army pulled my car over, hauled me out of the car and broke every hurley I had, throwing them over the ditch. And you could do nothing about it. We were playing a championship match for the club, about a mile away from the crowd and they held us back for over two and a half hours and there was three of our back line down the road in the rain, where they weren't allowed to play. That sort of thing was normal.

'Back in the day with the UDR [Ulster Defence Regiment]

you had to vary your way to work and things like that. I got a bullet through the post with a letter that said, "The next time your name will be in the newspaper it'll be in the death column." That's the environment we came from. Hurling was more than just a game to us.'

You sense he could talk for hours about incidents and memories of being a hurling man during the Troubles, but somehow, Sambo believes, you can't let the bitterness take hold. You have to find a way to deal with it and get on with your life. Looking back, you can try to make sense of it all, while the generation who grew up with the Good Friday Agreement probably wouldn't even know what the UDR stands for. They're gone, times are different and, thankfully, things are different now too. Now you can wear a GAA jersey in public, walk through a shopping centre and not feel like you're going to be threatened.

The reason it also meant more to Sambo and his fellow hurlers in Antrim was that they were training as hard as any-one else in the country, but knew in their hearts they would never have a realistic chance of winning an All-Ireland.

Antrim, Sambo's own county, is the hotbed of hurling in the province. The Glens on the coast in the north-east, looking across to Scotland, have always been strongly linked to stick games in one shape or another, with shinty being the Scottish equivalent. While most of the Ulster counties were focused on Gaelic football, it was in pockets of Antrim (and in Derry), in places such as the Glens, Cushendall and Ballycastle, that hurling survived. These small areas have acted as frontiers of hurling surrounded not only by Gaelic football but by other sporting cultures entirely.

Antrim is the only Ulster county to have made it as far as the All-Ireland final: the first time in 1943 when they were beaten by the famous Cork four-in-a-row team, and the second time in 1989 when Tipp beat them in a facile eighteen-point victory McNaughton played in. This was the highlight of his seventeen years playing for Antrim, from 1981 to 1997.

Before the backdoor system was created, at least Antrim (or whoever were the Ulster champions) could expect an All-Ireland quarter-final or semi-final to look forward to, but since the championship opened up to losing teams from Leinster and Munster, the likes of Antrim have found it increasingly hard to keep up.

The sport has to be more deeply ingrained for it to survive in these pockets of communities. While kids love to play sport, hurling is a hard game to coach, McNaughton points out, compared to the likes of soccer or Gaelic football. It's easier for a coach to say, 'Give me four footballs' and away you go.

'It's not that we didn't like Gaelic football, we just never really played it that much. We've always been hurling people,' says McNaughton.

His three kids, Terri-Marie, Shane and Christy have all followed in their father's footsteps, with Shane having played for the Antrim senior team, Christy on the minors and Terri-

Marie playing camogie for Cushendall. 'Even the dog hurls!' McNaughton says.

He views hurling and hurling people almost in a spiritual sense. To be a good hurler you have to first be a good person.

'You need certain qualities. You need commitment, you need to be good on a team, you need honesty. All of these things make you a good person. If you've got commitment and you have honesty in a person, they're usually heading towards being a good person.

'To be part of something bigger than yourself, when you can be outspoken and disagree but if you look across the room and even though you know that fella's a cheeky bastard, he's going to back me later on. It's about you going in with a frame of mind that you're going to leave the place better than you found it or at least equally as good as you found it.'

To describe Sambo as just a 'hurling person' is to under-estimate the importance of this sport in his life. Ruairí Ógs in Cushendall was his club from the time that, when he was a kid, a hurley was placed in his hand and he was handed his future in the form of a length of ash and a sliotar. He was only sixteen when he was called up to the county senior team, and played for Antrim for the next seventeen years, which in-cluded six Ulster titles and an All-Ireland appearance, as well as an All Star award. He was to epitomise Antrim hurling in every way during this period, with not only his skill, but more so, his dedication to the cause. After seventeen years playing, he was never going to just walk away from it all.

'I developed a great love for the game and a love for the club and a passion for my county. If you've got character and passion, it's hard to play for a team for seventeen years and walk away. How do you do that? If they asked you to help, it's hard not to help. I've always found that, although there's times that I'd be saying "That's me done", [and then] I'm back again. There's part of it out of plain loyalty and also just being out there on the sideline.'

So much so that he's returned as manager of Antrim again. Seeing the dire state the county was in he couldn't stay away any longer. His first period in charge as co-manager with Dominic 'Woody' McKinley lasted three seasons, from 2007 to 2009, with successive Ulster titles but little success in the All-Ireland qualifiers, although they did win the early season Walsh Cup in 2008, famously beating Kilkenny along the way.

However, Antrim seniors have been beaten by hurling minnows Meath in recent years, while their minors and U-21s were regularly losing by twenty points.

'When the call came, I couldn't see my own county disintegrate. I'm disappointed the situation has developed to where it is. When I was hurling, we were trying to close a gap to the Corks, Tipperarys and Galways. Now we're trying to close the gap to the Westmeaths and Laois. How did it get to this situation? That's what I want to fix.'

When he confirmed he was taking over for a second stint, along with selectors Dominic McKinley, Gary O'Kane and

Neal Peden, McNaughton told Martin Breheny of the *Irish Independent*, 'It's embarrassing. But then what can you expect? There's no point having the U-21s and minors going straight into the All-Ireland semi-finals or quarter-finals because they're not ready for it. There was a time when we had minors who were ready for it but not now.'

The struggles for Antrim hurling are particularly acute. They're fighting an uphill battle compared to the bigger counties who have some success or 'glamour' associated with their teams.

For McNaughton it's also about bringing hurling back as a game of the people and by the people. He doesn't believe 'outside' managers can truly grasp the inner workings or desire of a county and its players. They're not there twenty-four/seven, they don't know every player, he says. 'You need to be at the club games and see all that is going on.'

He also points to struggles and politics at county-board level, which have affected the running of the Antrim team, and to an 'us versus them' element which has developed.

'The good people in the clubs ran back to their clubs and stayed there and when someone walked away [from the inter-county set-up], nobody wanted to get involved because things weren't being done right. You weren't getting any tools to do the job.'

He points to the period in the early 2000s when he was Antrim's minor manager as a time when they were given the tools to do the job properly. They had matches against the likes of Liam Sheedy's Tipperary minors and were getting their players up to the pace and level of what was required. It was when the teams stopped going south to play others at this level that he saw the falling-off in standards.

'You'll not tell me a seventeen-year-old in Galway is any different to a seventeen-year-old in the North. Their lives are the same whether they're doing their schoolwork, they're falling out with their dad, they've got a girlfriend, whatever. Plus, their skill level is the same. A guy from Antrim can strike a ball the same as a guy in Galway, but the difference is being able to do it under pressure and at pace. That's the key difference.

'We proved, in the 2000s, that, once we were given the tools to do the job, we could compete. The Galway team who won an All-Ireland beat us by two points; Limerick stole a game off us in Parnell Park. We could, if we had better luck, have had two minor All-Irelands.'

But without any tangible success, without any heroes for kids to look up to, without any publicity or PR to sway the kids' attention, where, he asks, is the light at the end of the tunnel for an Antrim hurler growing up? What have they to aim for?

McNaughton points to 1989 as a missed opportunity for the county, not only in the manner of the All-Ireland final defeat, but in not grasping the qualities and standards to influence future generations.

McNaughton doesn't make excuses for the eighteen-point defeat which left a sour taste for a long time, but he also points to the fact that they had absolutely no experience of All-Ireland final day, didn't know what to expect and were completely out of their comfort zone.

'Looking back on it, the things we prepared for that game, we had no experience with an All-Ireland and we were caught up in hype. We forgot about the hurling match. Before we couldn't get a fucking sandwich and then people were giving us jackets and free boots and all that sort of thing. Reporters were coming, there were interviews, TV cameras, and people forgot about the team and the real reason we were in the final in the first place.'

He's convinced it was mindset and mentality that made the difference, although nobody could accuse McNaughton of not following his own mind. In the run-up to the 1989 final the team's sports psychologist recommended he bring some of the dirt from his local Cushendall pitch with him to throw it down on the Croke Park sod and pretend he was just playing at home. 'Why would I do that?' he asked incredulously. His dream since he was a kid was to play in Croke Park. 'I can play on my club pitch any day of the week, I want to play in Croke Park!' Suffice to say no Cushendall dirt was spread that final day.

McNaughton was a player with great self-belief and he has the same belief in many of the Antrim hurlers as well.

'Twelve Antrim players would be every bit as good. If you take away the superstars, the likes of D. J. Carey or Henry

Shefflin, and if you analyse it, their teammates wouldn't have got the prizes without those superstar players alongside them.'

Strength in depth in terms of playing numbers is also always an issue. One or two injuries and the likes of Antrim can't compete, especially if club campaigns then become a priority.

What hurts now, looking back from where Antrim were in the late 1980s/early 1990s to where they are now, is the sense of a massive opportunity having been missed.

'What we could have done with the heights that we had reached at that time, that was never utilised, or the goodwill that the people had towards us. There were buses leaving from every valley and from Belfast, they were coming from all over supporting us. Now you could take the whole support in the back of your car.

'You'll hear some people in Ulster saying that it's great to see the likes of Armagh and Tyrone improving, coming close to Antrim,' he told the *Irish Independent*'s Breheny on 25 August 2016. 'The reality is that we've gone back to their level and that's no good to us or to hurling. But does anyone outside Antrim care? Do they care if we fall away altogether? You'd wonder sometimes. We're not looking for hand-outs, just genuine support to help the game in a county where there's real passion for it. Hurling will be the loser if Antrim doesn't come back.'

Looking back, he says, there's always some reason or excuse why they're not there at the highest level of the game. He feels there's no place for excuses.

'Sometimes you need to look in the mirror if you have a problem. You need to really analyse. You need to be honest with yourself. There's no point in listening to the guy at the end of the bar because he's telling you what you want to hear. Sometimes you might have to have uncomfortable truths told to you as a player: "I don't like what the coach is saying but he has a fucking point. I can't catch a ball or I can't do this"'.

An attitude and a failing that he sees in a lot of modern players is that there's too much pointing the finger and laying the blame for a team's failings on the manager. But, McNaughton believes, more soul-searching is needed, stronger characters to stand up and drive on regardless, much like what they had around the 1989 period.

'That was a team of very courageous, very strong-minded people, very much individual people in a sense that they would stand alone for their beliefs. We were united and we developed a bond that the majority of us have to this day. If you train hard together and you work together, it gives you a good self-satisfaction that you're part of something.

'It's human nature, the majority of people love to be part of something. We all love to be part of a family, love to be part of a community, club, whatever it is. If you're part of something that you see everybody around you is wanting the same thing and we're all prepared to do that work to get it, it becomes very contagious. It becomes a drug.'

It's that sense of the collective, togetherness and accepting responsibility as a team that he wants to see return to Antrim hurling. In contrast to other inter-county managers he's not selling the dream of playing on the first Sunday in September at the start of the year. It's just not part of the reality for them and so to drive on regardless needs a special type of person.

'I'm a great believer, no matter what you do in life – whether it's being a father, marriage, going to work, being a boss, being an employee – you need commitment no matter what you do. If you want to be successful cutting the grass, you have to be out there doing it. No matter what it is, you have to commit to doing it.'

The problem for the last few years, as he sees it, has been distractions and sideshows. Too many 'star players' being ac-commodated and a 'drop-in centre' mentality being accepted.

'Sometimes we try to put the roof on the house before there's a foundation in place. You must get the foundations right first. There hasn't been a ball struck yet but I have to try and get the foundations of commitment, honesty – old-fashioned values – from the players. It's not that I'm a dinosaur because I'm not. I know there's a place for sports science and I generally believe there's better hurlers playing now than ever there was and that's due to sports science.'

But what's the use of science and stats if it's built on sand, McNaughton wonders. Antrim hurling is in a bad place, he says, and the answers he tries to give to my queries about it are more than just black-and-white explanations. It runs deeper and is more complex than that.

'It's not easy for me to sit here and hold my heart out to

a complete stranger about Antrim hurling. For you to ask me a simple question, is it because of such and such? No, it's because of numerous things.'

As a manager preparing for the new season there are, though, priorities that he has to nail down and get right for the squad. He has to find the right mix of players, the right type of personalities who will go through walls to succeed for Antrim. Commitment and honesty have to be above and beyond; egos and other diseases that infect a team like a cancer have to be obliterated.

Before, the team might have stood like the derelict house left alone for years. You walked by it every day and the windows were all intact. Then one day one window is broken, and within the next couple of weeks every window in that house is broken. Pretty soon it's a broken shell.

'That's what ego is and that's what can happen on a team. I've seen it and watched it develop.'

McNaughton wants to rebuild the house and at the slightest hint of any stone throwers or windows being broken, he will be coming down on them like a tonne of bricks. He bristles, though, at the notion that managers were just about shouting and anger when he was a player. He sees it as a disservice to the quality of managers that existed.

'It wasn't as if they were kicking down doors and throwing stuff around. There were intelligent people then too. There were times you had to rise up and change things obviously. There were times when it was overheated and the manager lost it, but most times, the manager would come in and say, "This is what we're doing wrong, we need to be doing this instead."'

It's the players and their mindsets that have changed, he says. It's about being able to pull a player aside and say, 'Listen, this is how you defend' or, 'This is how you block' and they listen, take it in and are thankful for the instruction.

Nowadays McNaughton sees an inability on the part of players to take criticism.

'You don't like what I say? You're going to go and tell your mother. You're going to go home and tell her, "He's always picking on me", and the mother's like, "Ah, the culture's so negative." And yet, parents come up to me and say, "John won't work hard enough." I'm trying to tell them, these aren't negatives the kids are being told by us, it's what they need to work on.

'Is he hooking or blocking, or is he working harder? Maybe, maybe not, but nobody wants to hear their own son being criticised, nobody wants to hear how they need to improve. It's all about social media now, it's all about how many fucking friends you have on Facebook. You've got five hundred friends on Facebook? And four of them turn up at your funeral? Society's all about how many tweets you get, needing to be led, needing to be someone's friends. The majority of us didn't give a fuck, maybe because we grew up in an Ireland where constant fucking guns were wrecking homes out there.'

There's a passion and an anger that rises up at times in McNaughton. It's a derision of softness, of social media, of attention-seeking, which, he believes, smothers everything that's really of value in people, starting with honesty and commitment. But he also accepts that kids nowadays won't have the same values or experiences that he did growing up.

'I grew up on a farm and I used to have to take an air rifle to the outdoors toilet to shoot the rats. We thought that was the norm. I remember me Dad taking blue mould off the bread and then toasting it. My kids wouldn't know what fucking blue mould is. If they saw blue mould on a bread they'd wonder, "Is that a new type of bread?"'

Society has created individuals that are weaker mentally, he says. When players buckle under the pressure and miss easy frees to win finals, or when teams can't hold onto leads, that's mental weakness, he says.

He does believe in the player power that can see managers ousted, however, and sees it as a strength that the good players have. It's becoming more common, from Cork to Galway and Clare. From McNaughton's experience as a player, some managers simply weren't good enough to bring players to the next level.

'Everything's great when you're winning, but can the manager create an environment where bullshit doesn't succeed? There's players in Kilkenny that you have never heard of, who didn't cut it because they didn't have the commitment or character. You never hear of them but they're there. They're very talented, very skilful players but they just don't come to the surface, they play in their clubs and they dip in and out.'

It's the culture of bullshit that he most has an issue with in Antrim hurling. Somebody has to step forward to stop it from developing any further. Somebody has to change the culture.

'Someone has to take it seriously; we have to stop what's gone on for the past twenty years. Antrim hurling these past twenty years has been like a drop-in centre. You'll see people going to America, people going to England, going back and forth like it was a drop-in centre.'

It's the apathy, the take it or leave it approach which is anathema to him. If you're a hurler in Antrim how can it not mean more? How can you not want to be better?

'You have to want to play against a better standard to become better. You have to be ambitious. That's a good word: ambitious. Instead of being egotistical, be ambitious. Be a glory hunter. There's nothing wrong in being a glory hunter, wanting more for yourself and to better yourself. Kids want to score goals, want to be good at sports and that sort of player can develop that sort of ambitious culture.'

The targets he has as a manager at the start aren't targets on the pitch. Second-tier competitions like the Christy Ring Cup are pointless, he says, if the foundations haven't been laid down. He needs players in the dressing room for the right reasons in the first place, where everybody is committed to the cause.

'Antrim will never go anywhere till we stop looking in the car park to see who's going to turn up. That's my number one priority, that we stop looking in the fucking car park, that we know who's going to turn up, that we know everybody there is with us.

'I have to see who's going to be with me every day. I don't have to look in the car park. Then you can sit down and start worrying about the hurling. But hurling is secondary at the moment in the winter. I'm worried about the kind of person first.

'We're not in a good place but if we get the foundations in place we can stop the rot and move forward again. It's not going to happen in my management, maybe. Hopefully we'll improve. We'll come up and then we'll improve.'

Who knows where it all might end up, I laugh – Antrim versus Tipp again in an All-Ireland final?

'Well, you never know,' he says, allowing himself a smile. 'Who would have said Donald Trump would be fucking president of America?'

So what would be a successful tenure for McNaughton this time around?

'Success for me, if I walk away from this job, is if I've left it better than I found it, that everybody there is committed and the next manager has a foundation they can build on. He can then take it to another level. We've been in decline for roughly twenty years. Somebody has to say enough's enough here.

'In Ulster terms, hurling is seen as a hindrance to football, especially by club football managers. You can see it in Derry when the hurlers are playing Christy Ring and they put a football championship match on the night before. Now, you can talk about hurling men such as Brian Cody or Ger Loughnane, but they wouldn't have a clue what I'm talking about when I say hurling is a second-class sport in your county.'

Football in the big counties seems to be on a path that is ever-diverging from the rest. Plans for the Super 8 part of the championship from 2018 (a proposed new format for the championship whereby the four provincial champions and the four provincial runners-up, or the team that beats them in round four of the qualifiers, will play in two groups of four for a place in the All-Ireland semis) have drawn particular ire with club players, smaller counties and hurling people, who say it is elitist and will only help the bigger counties get better and get more exposure.

Dublin's success of recent years has also thrown a light on the impact of professional-level training and preparation.

'I met a guy from Dublin and you know what his job is? Delivering water to Dublin footballers and hurlers. That's what his day job is. He goes into their workplace delivering water so they keep themselves hydrated. I mean, how can you compete with that?

'The reality for me and the Antrim hurlers is we're not going to get expenses for certain things and we're not getting fed after [training and games] because we can't afford it. In two months I'd say I've done 3,000 miles. I don't get any expenses for them. Nothing. When we meet, we're not allowed to even order a cup of coffee at the hotel.'

Meanwhile, over the winter months, he's chasing and harassing colleges and clubs for pitches they can train on. Phone call after phone call, seeing if they can cut a deal and make a booking.

From eight in the morning to last thing at night he's on the phone to his selectors, 'You do this, I'll do that and I'll do this', doing the job of a backroom team practically by himself. There are fundraisers to be organised, tickets to sell, money to collect. He's even taking part in a white-collar boxing event to help raise the funds. It would be hard to picture Brian Cody selling tickets for and then taking part in a boxing match.

'Being a manager, it's a real fucking dream,' he says with a wry smile.

But there's no other place he would be, and at least there have been improvements with a good board now involved helping out: 'There was a coup last year and good people are there for the right reasons.'

Then there's the training, the costs and the effort needed just to keep at a certain level.

'I'm asking our guys to basically put in the same effort as the top counties. To try and close that gap I have to bring in the same effort. If I only train two nights a week and you're training four nights a week, chances are we're not going to close the gap. I have to at least match the others.

'You have to have all these boxes ticked so it's not an issue. You have to have your dietician, you have to have your strength and conditioning coach, you have to have your psychologist, you have to have your kit man, your doctors and your physios. Dietician, nutritionist, what's the difference? I've asked people that one and can somebody please tell me the difference? Maybe this is me being uneducated but the problem is, if you don't have them all are you doing something wrong?'

McNaughton thinks hurling is swinging too much towards science nowadays and if somebody sees something from one sport they all have to have it or be doing it.

'The rugby teams are warming up on their bikes before coming on and now the Antrim hurlers have to have their bikes.'

Having travelled all over Ireland to watch teams train, picking people's brains, he brings it back to Kilkenny and their approach as to what you can really learn from a team.

'They do seven different drills, seven different roles where you're learning one thing each time. All you're doing is strike and touch, strike and touch.'

They've also built up a culture that's the envy of the rest of the country, not just Antrim, where everyone buys into what is needed to succeed, even down to the fundraising. Once when he was at a Kilkenny training session he saw Eddie Keher, one of the legends of the game, standing on a box collecting money for the team and there was a queue to the far end of the ground wanting to contribute.

Nobody is above the jersey and it's about leaving the jersey better than you found it. The New Zealand rugby team have a similar ethos, 'Better people make better All Blacks'.

It's a philosophical approach to the game and to the county that might surprise some when thinking of Sambo McNaughton. He's an avid reader of books on leaders and management and, in the evening, to switch off from the day, he takes the dog out to the fields, puts the headphones on and lets his mind soak up teachings from the likes of John Wooden and Nelson Mandela.

For someone juggling work running a pub, family life and hurling management, audio books have been a godsend. When he picked up Mandela's autobiography, *A Long Walk to Freedom*, trying to figure out all the African names did his head in and he threw the book into the corner in frustration. His wife, however, signed him up to Audible, an audiobook service, to listen to the book instead and he doesn't have to worry about difficult African names any more. On his walks around Cushendall he's learning about the struggles of the African National Congress (ANC) and Mandela's endurance behind bars. You could take poetic licence at this point and compare McNaughton's lifetime of struggles for Antrim hurling to a lifetime on Robben Island, but he'd tell you to cop yourself on.

He'd perhaps prefer a comparison to John Wooden (whose book accompanied him in the car on the way to Dublin for this interview), the legendary American basketball coach who won ten National Collegiate Athletic Association championships in twelve years with University of California, Los Angeles in the 1960s and 1970s.

A philosophy built on decency doesn't have to be soft and Wooden's legacy was based around the 'Pyramid of Success', which, he claimed, made up the foundations upon which to build success in life and sport. At its base are industriousness, friendship, loyalty, cooperation and enthusiasm, all traits that McNaughton identifies with strongly. Above these include: self-control, alertness, initiative, intentness, team spirit, skill, condition, confidence and poise; competitive greatness is at the very top.

While Wooden was also a devout Christian, his religion didn't stop him from being tough – 'He comes across as a bit of a Holy Roller, but he wasn't a bit, he wasn't Mother Teresa, he was a fucking asshole too,' says McNaughton. 'You have to be tough to succeed in sport. You can show respect or good qualities but you have to be ruthless too if you want to achieve and if the team wants to achieve.'

The influence of Wooden is clear when one goes in-depth with McNaughton on the importance of foundations and embedding a culture and mindset that is long-lasting.

'If you're true to yourself you're going to be true to everyone else,' is one of Wooden's famous quotes, which fits very well as a mantra for McNaughton's hurling and managerial life.

His role as manager doesn't necessarily have to be with the inter-county senior team, but once it involves hurling with Antrim or Cushendall at any age group, he'll be true to himself and look to bring others along with him.

'At least if you're standing on the sideline and you're getting frustrated or you're getting beat and you've emotions of joy, despair, anger out there, it's easy to know you're alive. At least I still know that …'

11

The Mind:
EAMON O'SHEA

Listen to what it sounds like when the sliotar hits the back of the net. Listen closely – what does that sound like?

Just like Cork's John Allen, Tipperary's Eamon O'Shea was a reluctant inter-county manager. 'I never thought I would be involved in coaching and certainly not a manager,' he says, 'so I never had any aspirations to sort of do anything like that, I was just interested in playing.'

He was certainly interested in reading and soaking up as much information as possible, but that was a given, considering his background in academia and research. Sport was a passion that he also happened to read up on, whether it was Rinus Michels' 'Total Football' or other sporting influences. 'But I never put two and two together that I might do this. I was just interested in approaches, that was all.'

He has described himself as a 'different hurler than maybe

was in north Tipperary at the time', an 'esoteric' player. And he's right; there weren't many pucking about on the hurling fields of Kilruane who would end up researching dementia and its effects on society. He wasn't the 'robust' type of hurler who would be expected to survive the cut and thrust of Tipperary's club hurling scene in the 1980s.

But he had an enlightened manager in Len Gaynor (a Tipp star in the 1960s who went on to manage Clare and Tipperary), who appreciated that O'Shea brought something different to the field. Kilruane MacDonaghs, O'Shea's club, already had strong players, 'leaders of men all over the pitch'. O'Shea had something else to bring.

'I wouldn't have been the type of player that Len would immediately gravitate towards, but I remember him saying one day that my job was to pick up the pieces around the place and to make sure I was there when the ball was breaking. I had to make sure I was quick onto that ball, picked it up and moved it on.

'What Len said to me really struck me at the time because you feel the guy values you, even though you know he might think you're a different type of hurler.

'One of the few times I excelled at club level, I had won a man of the match award at a county final and I was very pleased with myself. I scored 1–04, something like that, so I thought he might congratulate me on the goal, but Len comes over to me and says, "That was a great tackle you made, to win that ball." It was very much a case of the other stuff is what you should be doing, but you did something above and beyond what you normally do and he had a great sense of making you feel part of something really good.'

It was an approach similar to what John Allen has described as not remembering any managers' speeches, but instead remembering how they made you feel. It's also the mark of any great manager that they can accommodate different types of players and personalities within a team.

Hurling was (and is) the universal language in Kilruane. It bound everyone across class, intelligence and background. It brought them together onto common ground. The hurling narrative was constant and would be struck up immediately, even if you had been away for years. Meeting people on the street, the talk wasn't of the economy or politics, it was always about the hurling, woven into the fabric of rural villages.

There's always the danger, of course, of looking back on those 'simpler' days through sepia-tinted glasses, O'Shea acknowledges. Life was tougher in many ways in the 1970s and 1980s, but the 'distracting noise' intruding into daily living wasn't there either. The modern world of digital connectivity, smartphones, emails and social media is bombarding us with information and updates that maybe we don't really need. We can read about a person's experience in Michigan just as easily as someone from down the road, but how much of it is really necessary? After all, we only have a limited ability to process it. In the pre-Internet days, you could at least leave it all behind.

The only noise for O'Shea growing up was hurling and study. Despite making it onto Tipp teams first as minor and then as senior from 1979 to 1986, he admits that, as a player, he just didn't work hard enough at it and always had other things on his mind.

His was the enquiring, wandering mind, soaking up different elements from soccer, with the Dutch side Ajax, and even Shamrock Rovers, to basketball and Gaelic football. And there was the study – economics at UCD – a subject that fascinated him from a philosophical and human perspective.

He went on to specialise in ageing, writing over fifteen books on it, with dementia an area of particular interest. He wanted to focus on people and how society can best serve some of those affected with conditions such as dementia. For O'Shea, it's about connecting and finding the person within, and this has so many parallels to sport, the dressing room and the team.

The only surprise then was that coaching or management was not something that interested him after he stopped playing. His interest in sport and hurling didn't wane, but his involvement at a senior level did. While he'd be helping out with his club, it was only ever as an aside to his studies and work.

The fact that the Tipperary county team came calling in 2007, by which time he was fifty, makes it all the more remarkable. Liam Sheedy had been appointed manager in the wake of Babs Keating's departure and was looking for a coach, someone to help run the ship in terms of training and stra-

tegy. O'Shea's name came on the radar. It was Sheedy thinking outside the box, looking for something and someone a bit
different.

Eamon knew Liam's brother, John, and so discussions
were arranged. Sheedy elaborated on what he wanted and the
vision he had for Tipp. It tallied with O'Shea's and he knew
he wouldn't be wasting his time and that Sheedy would let
him do his job. And so, he was on board. The job was simple:
make sure the team played in a certain way.

'Once I knew what he wanted, I just said okay this is how
I'm going to do it.'

But why get involved in the first place?

'Because I had wanted to see could I influence something.'

Part of Sheedy's management ability was being able to
trust those to whom he had delegated responsibility, and
for the next three years O'Shea's role was clear and the trust
implicit.

'The great thing about Liam was, Liam just trusted the
relationship between the coach and manager. We had a
fantastic relationship, we have a fantastic relationship.

'What Liam brought was a really intense belief and he
communicated that belief to the players. If that belief hadn't
been communicated to the players my job would have been
much harder. It was my job to ensure that that belief was
manifested in the way we played.'

The last time O'Shea had been involved with an inter-
county team was over twenty years beforehand, when he was

still playing, but coming in to the team didn't phase or intimidate him. He had been helping some players individually who were at NUI Galway, where O'Shea was doing research work, and was aware of the current thinking and developments in the game. Coming in to Tipp, he knew what he had to do, and the management team shared a vision and philosophy for how to do it.

The days of sweeper systems were still a few years off and for O'Shea it was something of a blank canvas. For sure the objective was to win the All-Ireland, but at the same time, it had to be about a lot more than that. It had to run deeper.

'My belief would be that you have to try and influence something that's more long-term and sustainable, and fits into, as a coach or a manager, my view of the world. So, if we're trying to develop leaders and are trying to develop people, we have got to organise training and the philosophy in the dressing room around a creation of independence.'

Reaching out to individuals for the greater good is as good a philosophy as any to bring to any walk of life, and it was particularly beneficial for the Tipperary hurling set-up. O'Shea may have been different to what went before, but that didn't mean he was going to change his style or thinking.

'The players have got to believe in you. So as long as you are being you, the players will believe in you. It's not necessarily saying you're going to be successful, but the players will keep believing in you as long as you are not trying to be something you're not.'

Brendan Cummins wrote in his autobiography, *Standing My Ground*, of the influence that O'Shea had on the players: 'I found him a little eccentric at first, but once you started to understand what he was trying to get you to do, how he wanted to open your mind to creative possibilities in how you played, you were soon a different and better player ... Bland wasn't good enough. If you're bland, you might as well be a lemming running off a cliff with the rest of them. Socially conditioned to follow the pack rather than stand out from the crowd.'

'When I looked at the team,' explains O'Shea, 'I wanted Tipp to play in a particular way and I wanted them to lead. I wanted to get back to what I call "pure hurling", relying on movement, on striking, and relying on all the things that I thought these players had. Once Liam believed in it, we didn't have to talk very much. He knew that I could do this and I was happy that's what he wanted.'

The manager-coach dynamic is an important one and it worked for Sheedy and O'Shea because, although they shared the same philosophy, they came at it from different perspectives.

For a start, Sheedy was a defender whereas O'Shea was a forward. A manager's playing background can sometimes be overlooked when it comes to their philosophy and approach in later years, but it's no coincidence that many defensive-minded systems would have come from players who were once defenders, while forwards brought a lot more creativity and expansiveness to their vision of the game.

Michael Ryan as selector (and future All-Ireland-winning manager) was the other part of Sheedy's triumvirate. Their ongoing discussions throughout the year influenced each other in conscious and subconscious ways.

'Mick and Liam would have influenced me saying, "No, that's too pure." They wouldn't say this is how it should be done, but they would say, "Okay, that's too pure, you need to rein it in."'

One of the first things O'Shea introduced to the training sessions was getting the players to use their senses more, especially the sense of hearing. Sounds are very subjective and personal but can also bring us much closer to our environments if we stop and focus on what we're listening to. It was a unique approach and way of thinking. Often he made the players stand on the training pitch in front of him, even before any physical training was done.

'Listen to the goal,' he would tell them. 'Listen to what it sounds like when the sliotar hits the back of the net. Listen closely – what does that sound like?'

It's a fascinating approach and way of thinking, highlighting the importance of being sensitised to movement, the other players, the field and the ball. When this awareness comes together in any sport, be it soccer, rugby or hurling, that is when the players are tuned in the most.

The senses, sounds and the feel of the ball are perhaps not common aspects of Gaelic games that people in the GAA talk about (too esoteric perhaps?) but, as O'Shea emphasises,

'The ball is the critical thing. It's not rocket science, it's just going back and getting the feel of the hurley and the feel of the ball again, talking to them about this and what they're feeling, what they're seeing, what they're hearing.'

His different approach also highlights the wider understanding and thinking in his background.

'It's in here,' he says, pointing to his head. 'It's the way I think about the world. When I take a hurley in my hand it's just an extension of me. I feel this is the most natural thing, the same as golfers or tennis players. So you are just trying to be at one with what you are doing.

'I don't consider it any way novel in the sense that this is what we do. These boys travel with their hurleys everywhere, so really it is just trying to say, this is something that you don't even have to think about, we want to take advantage of this, this is what you are, you're a hurler. So therefore if you are a hurler we try to maximise every aspect of that relationship. Even their strike is all about sound.'

Those ten minutes at the start of training are vital, explaining to the players what they're doing, why they're there and making sure they're all of one mind in the concept, getting them into this headspace.

'I would take them up to the goals and say, "Do you hear that?" And they would say, "What?"

'I said, "Can you hear it now?" I would strike a ball into the net and the net would move ever so slightly but the forwards would hear it and the backs wouldn't because it's in the mentality of a forward to want to hear a sound like that.

'You don't actually hear the sound when the ball hits the net, but because of the way you train, what's conjured up is [the desire that] "This is what I want to hear." When you are telling them I want you to put the ball a foot inside the post because that's where it hurts most when it goes in, they are thinking, okay, I see it, as it's part of visualisation but now I also feel it. And that's almost imperceptible but also very personal.'

As for defenders?

'I usually made a joke that the defenders only hear the thud of when you take somebody out of the game. But it is also about sound then, it's about the catch and it's about the clearance.'

Spatial understanding is also key, especially in team sports and fast-moving ones, but when players would ask him about it, his response was that it's only something they can understand themselves because what they see is in their own heads and their own minds.

'When you reach back for a catch, you get pressure immediately, and immediately you brace yourself for the tackle, but then when you look up there's still so much space ahead of you.

'When you look up, I can't tell you where to hit the ball, you have got to have all that figured out as to what the guy up there that you are trying to hit at number fourteen is thinking. You've got to put the ball into the best place you possibly can, so space is actually your creation.

'We would do a lot of stuff just looking at the pitch. We would do random plays, moving things about, and then we would say, "Okay, stop. What do you see when you look up there? Where do you see the spaces opening up? Where do you want to put the ball?"'

There's no formula to acquiring a better understanding of space, he says, it's more implicit rather than anything else and becomes part of the collective way of thinking and playing.

Focusing on the senses and the internal subjective experience of the players was part of O'Shea's vision, and whilst different, it certainly had an impact and made a difference.

'The great thing was the players bought into it and also accepted failure sometimes as part of it. I probably wouldn't have stayed very long if they hadn't bought into it. I would have been aware that if I could make a contribution here I will stay, if I can't make a contribution then I am not going to waste everyone's time.'

In those three years under Sheedy's management, Tipp regained and retained Munster (their first provincial title since 2001) and reached two All-Ireland finals, but couldn't stop Kilkenny as the Cats made it a record-equalling four-in-a-row in 2009. The following year, though, would be pivotal in both counties' histories.

Kilkenny were going for an unprecedented five-in-a-row, a feat never achieved before in either hurling or Gaelic football. Tipp, their great rivals, had to ensure it didn't happen. And they did, in style, scoring 4–17 to Kilkenny's 1–18, running out eight-point winners. It was the biggest score Kilkenny had conceded in a seventy-minute final and Lar Corbett was the first player since Cork's Eddie O'Brien in 1970 to score a hat-trick in an All-Ireland final. Hearing the sound of the net rippling all those nights in training had paid off when it mattered the most.

Time and work commitments meant Liam Sheedy stepped down in the wake of Tipp's triumph and Eamon O'Shea followed suit. Their three years together had established a vision and a philosophy for Tipperary hurling to build upon.

Declan Ryan, Tipp's successful minor manager, succeeded Sheedy in late 2010 and it appeared as if the team had lost none of their verve or style, scoring an incredible 7–19 against Waterford in the Munster final in 2011. But Kilkenny were waiting for the third final in a row and got their own revenge, recapturing Liam MacCarthy with a four-point win.

In 2012 Tipperary were again victorious in Munster and were again beaten by Kilkenny, this time in the All-Ireland semi-final and by a humiliating eighteen points. Declan Ryan stepped down after two years in charge and Tipp returned to what was familiar in 2013 when Eamon O'Shea was appointed manager.

This time, however, the relationship was to be different. No longer the coach taking them through training and practice on the field, he was now the manager, the delegator. Whilst the hurling philosophy and belief in a positive, attacking approach remained, in the two years since he had stepped down as coach, the game had changed, with more defensive systems having been introduced.

'When I went back it took me a little while to think – do you know what, teams are playing differently against us now. Systems had evolved and the minutiae of the play had evolved very quickly. I can understand why people use the sweeper system and I can understand teams who have a tradition of winning not using it. If you look at other teams, and they haven't won an All-Ireland in a lot of years, I can see why they may be looking to have another way of approaching things. Even if the game evolved there's nothing wrong with thinkers involved in the game who want to play a particular way.

'Having said all that, I don't believe hurling lends itself like football or rugby to that kind of structuredness. And I think we have been influenced by trainers and coaches who might be looking too closely at these other sports and therefore influencing the way we think about the game.

'I don't see this as being traditionalist versus non-traditionalist. I see influences coming in that maybe, over time, the evidence will show that this was not the way to play the game to win. The game itself, in my view, is a unique game. I don't see it in a protectionist way, but it's unique in that it can't be measured as a tactical, strategic type of game.

'One of its great attractions is the randomness of the game in terms of the way the ball goes. The game is played with heart, soul and technique and I believe that there's a beat to all good hurling games. I hate watching a bad hurling game because it just undermines everything I believe in. There has to be a level of intensity, there has to be the rhythm, almost like a drum beat. There is an authenticity to the way the game is played. You can get that authenticity in a club match and it doesn't have to be super players on the pitch; we're not talking about elite level here, we are talking about an authenticity where it's all about "right, let's go".'

One passage of play that stands out for him from the 2014 Tipp-Kilkenny final is when there were three non-stop minutes of complete intensity and give and take: 'The amount of respect in those 180 seconds from players who were throwing their bodies in, up, down, up, down, up, down – I could watch games like that all the time. Especially because within that you can have technique, you can have movement, you can have everything you want, but the game has to be played at that kind of intensity, pace and authenticity which can be done at any level. I love to see an U-15 game or a minor game when it is hell for leather because, to me, that is the essence of the game. It mightn't be to other people but to me it is the essence of hurling.'

The systems being introduced when he returned to management were not just anathema to him but also to his players, and even if they had to try it out in training to prepare for the opposition, players would be frustrated saying, 'We can't do it, just can't.'

When they won Munster in his final year in charge, there was still frustration about the way they played and the fact no goals had been scored. At training the following week, players were saying there was something missing in their game and how they wanted to play.

They were determined to find a way around it and they did the next year, but they had to figure it out. The players were committed to an ongoing process of development and this is part of the reason why O'Shea, although stepping down after three years with no All-Irelands and a semi-final defeat to Galway in his last outing, was so optimistic when he left. The players, he knew, were really committed to this.

Another area of change was in the emphasis on stats and data. With O'Shea's background in economics, an evidence-based approach to the game would have come naturally to him. However, O'Shea refused to allow this newfound reliance on stats and data change his philosophy.

'As a manager there is a lot of pressure to make sure you are as data driven or as information savvy as the next manager,' he admits. 'But my philosophy is still that the ball needs to be got to the players who can play as quickly as possible and that hasn't changed.

'Everything is done to open up the space to create the environment where your top players, your really top players, can play. But it also means that one of the things that can happen in a game like Tipp used to play, is there can be a bit of self-indulgence, to show how good we are. Often we have had to say, no, no, that's not how we want to play here. It's too much. You need to get back. You need to play it real.

'Now, evidence is good, but the game in my view is different, because it can move from point A to point B, and because it is non-stop, you can look too much at the data and say, okay, so now we need to control the ball more, we need to hold onto the ball more, we need to move the ball sideways, then sideways again. When the data is determining how you play you are in trouble.

'The data should only back up your philosophy. So therefore you may be looking for things that I'm not looking for. When I was involved, you might say the data is showing we didn't make enough tackles or something like that, and I might be looking at something entirely different. The data is just there. You can find anything in data.'

Do the data and emphasis on stats make managers and teams more risk averse? You have to be careful raising such talking points with an academic versed in economics, as you will get references to behavioural economics and the works of Kahneman and Tversky thrown back at you, asking what risk is, why players are risk averse and how you get them to take more risks. A player will put more effort and energy into making sure he doesn't look bad, O'Shea explains.

'You might be trying to use some of these concepts as in the way you want to play. And then let them play the game as it evolves, but ensuring that they are also going to take some risks. If you look at the data in golf, for example, players take more time in trying to save pars than they do in trying to get birdies, because making pars means you are risk averse.

'So, would I take the same time and concentration over a birdie? No, I'll take more time and concentration over making sure I make a par. And that is all to do with risk, or their view of risk. So part of the issue I think in hurling is to make sure that we have as many risk lovers on the pitch as possible.'

Overall, most would agree that there is a happy balance to be struck, but it is refreshing to hear such arguments about the need for risk lovers in the modern game and, indeed, in modern society.

'If you make a mistake? You can try again of course! Or if you keep on trying it and you are not able to do it, well then I have to make a decision on this, on you as a player. But at the same time it is about that trust. When I look at a team that is what I want to see. I want to see this team is comfortable and confident in itself.'

One of the accusations thrown at the Tipperary players who won the All-Ireland in 2010 was that they should have won another soon after and should not have had to wait six years for their next title. It's something O'Shea accepts, but the development and learning curve of some of those players, who are now older and more experienced, means that in 2017 and beyond the Tipperary team is in a much better place for its evolution and development. Achieving consistent success has to be next in the process for them and Kilkenny are the standard-bearers for this.

'Now I would judge success as a couple of things: one is actually winning trophies, that's what the fans want. The other is that you have a sustainable and consistent and understandable way that you play that is inherently true to something you believe in.'

Liam Sheedy, Eamon O'Shea and Michael Ryan laid the foundations from 2008 to 2010 and, while Kilkenny's constant in the dressing room has been Brian Cody, they would like to think that, if the managers in Tipperary change, the philosophy and belief system that were instilled during their tenures will remain.

From 2010 on, however, O'Shea concedes that where Tipp were lagging behind Kilkenny was in the strength of leadership on the pitch. It's about developing that mentality right across the team.

'We had some incredibly strong leaders like Eoin Kelly who, certainly as a sportsman, would be one of the people that I would say has a mentality for the ages,' says O'Shea. 'But I think we could have done with more. And I think one of the things that those five or six players who won the All-Ireland in 2010 and who were also U-21 have now, is a serious mentality in the Tipperary set-up.'

Learning from experience is a key ingredient in developing that mental toughness and there's always a danger where players live and play in a bubble world of development squads, Fresher squads, county training and being lauded in their clubs, that the 'softness' as Ger Loughnane calls it, or the 'wipe-me-arse mentality' as Anthony Daly refers to it, can be reflected on the pitch when one's mettle is truly tested.

'I saw a rugby team recently in a hotel preparing for a game and I was thinking these guys must be bored out of their minds. They do this every week, everybody sitting there with their headphones on, and I was thinking, how do you actually develop as a professional sportsperson? And a lot of GAA at the upper level, it kind of mirrors that too. How do you ensure that these players are developed, making sure they are being stretched in different ways either intellectually or understanding people or the world?

'If you think about the Clare team, the 1990s team that won the All-Irelands, these players were outstanding individuals on their own merit. Even the guys who weren't physically strong, they were mentally strong. So I think that was part of the reason for their success.'

The years after 2010 have given Tipperary players an opportunity to evolve.

'The guys who are now in their later twenties are substantial men who have developed this mentality through trial and error, as well as through consideration and through discussion. These guys talk to each other now a lot more, which is absolutely critical.

'Some people talk about the manager who facilitates and there's an appetite out there for this vision of the manager who is very strong and has control over his players, and some of the most successful managers have done that in soccer, for example, when you take Ferguson.

'Brian Cody is often seen like this too, but I don't know

Brian Cody and I wonder about that. I see him on the sideline giving power to his players and his players expressing that on the pitch and I think it's really good to have the ability of those players to lead on the pitch. You don't get that if you have a manager who is all control.'

When O'Shea returned to the Tipp set-up as manager in 2013, it was with the sense of re-establishing a connection to what had begun under Liam Sheedy. Although it had never been his intention to go back, he felt that the ship needed steadying and the onus had to be pushed back to the players.

'There would have been, if anything, almost too much belief,' he says. 'I had to get them back to working, to figuring it out for themselves. It was about giving them a lot more responsibility which was a big part of my role as manager.'

As well as that, he now also had to deal with the minutiae and logistics of hotels, timing arrivals and departures, the little things that make up the job.

'I was thinking, the only thing I want to do here is to make sure these guys play exactly the way I want them to play and I would be impatient with all that other stuff.'

He brought in Paudie O'Neill as his coach, along with Mick Ryan as assistant manager. The skill of delegation was one of the first things he had to learn. It took a while to get used to, as it did for the players who once had O'Shea as their coach.

'If I was being critical about myself I would say that maybe sometimes as a coach I was involved too closely with the players. Sometimes that separation of player, coach and manager is difficult to achieve. When you are engaged very closely with the players and trying to work with them, it is slightly different and more difficult as manager.

'But players also respond very differently. The key thing is that players have to see that you are honest. If I was to come in as manager and take another personality shift and say okay guys you are dealing with something entirely different here, the players would look at it and say, I don't believe that really. So, I didn't change. Might it have benefited the team differently? Would we have won an All-Ireland? Who knows? And people find this difficult to believe, but I'm not too bothered about that.'

That's not to say that the defeats in his first year to Limerick in Munster or to Kilkenny in the qualifiers didn't hurt. Nor the three-point loss in the replayed All-Ireland final to Kilkenny in 2014, or the semi-final defeat to Galway the following season.

'My intensity to win, you can't judge from the outside,' he says. 'The team would have known how devastated I was when we didn't win. There is no sense that I could reconcile these losses, which I felt badly. It wasn't a case that I sought refuge in work or anything like that, but at the same time it wasn't easily found and one can't underestimate the impact that the project meant to me.'

As to the future? He has so many other interests to pursue, but sport will always occupy a part of his mind and his life.

For a few years it dominated as Tipperary sought a way back to the top of the hurling table. But be it hurling, economics or life, for O'Shea it's about being the best you can be from within and without.

'There's three elements to being a good hurler and person,' he says. 'One is intellect, however that is ascribed. I'm not talking about academic intellect – I mean intellect as being the ability to just engage. We are not talking about being measured in leagues or points or degrees here; it's an ability to be cognitively engaged, so if I am communicating with you that you understand.

'The second element is perseverance or resilience. I've seen PhD candidates in here who have failed because they didn't stay at it and got disillusioned. And I've seen times in my own life where I failed and then I said to myself, "You know you really should have stuck at it."

'And the third thing then is curiosity. If you get those three together you are going to make a good hurler.'

'There has to be the perseverance and resilience,' he emphasises. 'And that's what I like about the Tipperary team. They have been resilient and persevered and they have been curious to explore new ways to think and that's why, when all is said and done, I'd be happy.'

ACKNOWLEDGEMENTS

As ever, when it comes to writing a book, I'm amazed at the time that interviewees freely and willingly give. The hurling managers in this book were nothing but exceptional in allowing me to delve into the past, present and future of their sporting lives, and to get their thoughts on the state of hurling in general.

Their lives have been dedicated to an amateur sport for which the only gain was on the field of play, but in giving their time so freely they summed up their generosity of spirit when it comes to the GAA and hurling in particular.

My thanks must also go to Mary Feehan of Mercier Press, who saw, after some initial cul-de-sacs, the merits in exploring the philosophies and mindsets of hurling managers. Long may independent thinking as represented by publishers such as Mercier continue, and my thanks to all on the team for seeing the book through from concept to publication.

My editor, Noel O'Regan, as well as Wendy Logue, did a wonderful job in tightening the manuscript and making me see that much cannot be presumed in the reader's eye.

Thanks to my agent, Peter O'Connell who, after three books (and counting) is still fighting the fight and helping me to believe in the career of a writer.

Finally to my family. Once again I was absent in body and spirit for many days (especially in the evenings and at weekends) as I slowly made my way through the words, lines and pages.

My wife, Trina, has now become something of an expert in the finer points of hurling – something I'm sure she never expected as a consequence of our marriage! As always, I couldn't have done it without you.

To my boys, Ryan and Charlie, who refuse to take their Tipp jerseys off, I'm still hoping my Dublin background will somehow be an influence and that Santa will leave a different shade of blue under the tree this year. You teach me more about the joy of living every day we're together.

This book, *The Art of Hurling*, is about more than a game; it's about an approach and attitude to life common to all of the men interviewed here that reaches out into every strand of their daily interactions with family, friends and colleagues. Their shared approach to playing hurling and winning All-Irelands is just one more philosophy to live by, and it's something I hope I can live up to for many years to come.

INDEX

MERCIER PRESS

IRISH PUBLISHER - IRISH STORY

We hope you enjoyed this book.

Since 1944, Mercier Press has published books that have been
critically important to Irish life and culture. Books that dealt with
subjects that informed readers about Irish scholars, Irish writers,
Irish history and Ireland's rich heritage.

We believe in the importance of providing accessible histories and
cultural books for all readers and all who are interested in Irish
cultural life.

Our website is the best place to find out more information about
Mercier, our books, authors, news and the best deals on a wide
variety of books. Mercier tracks the best prices for our books online
and we seek to offer the best value to our customers.

Sign up on our website to receive updates and special offers.

www.mercierpress.ie
www.facebook.com/mercier.press
www.twitter.com/irishpublisher

Mercier Press, Unit 3b, Oak House, Bessboro Rd, Blackrock, Cork, Ireland